Shape Up Your Program!

tips, teasers, & thoughts for type trainers

Collected and compiled by

Margaret U. Fields and Jean B. Reid

C A P T

CENTER FOR APPLICATIONS OF PSYCHOLOGICAL TYPE, Inc
2815 NW 13th St, Suite 401 · Gainesville, FL 32609

Published by
The Center for Applications of Psychological Type, Inc.
2815 NW 13th Street, Suite 401
Gainesville, FL 32609
352.375.0160
www.capt.org

Printed in the United States of America.

ISBN 0-935652-50-7
ISBN 978-0-935652-50-5

All efforts have been made to credit the proper people or organizations in this compilation of exercises. Please send errors or notices of omissions to the publisher.

Table of Contents

Published by the Center for Applications of Psychological Type

Optional/Different Combinations

Resources

Published by the Center for Applications of Psychological Type

Acknowledgments

Over the past twenty years, the Myers-Briggs Type Indicator® assessment has become one of the most widely used organizational development tools of its kind. Expert trainers in the field of psychological type continue to use their knowledge and creativity to develop experiential exercises that teach people about the meaning and power of type. This book contains the work of some of these experts.

CAPT would like to acknowledge and thank the following authors who contributed exercises, tips, and quotes that made the publication of this book possible.

Kay Abella*	Gordon Lawrence
Scott Anchors	C. Waite Maclin
Gae Boyd	Pat Marr*
Susan Brock	Charles Martin
Tom Carskadon	Mary McCaulley
Susan Clancy	Elizabeth Murphy
Eve Delunas*	Isabel Briggs Myers
Larry Demarest	John Nechworth
Sue Dutton	Diane Payne
Margaret Fields	Judith Provost
Tom Golatz	Barbara Reid
Sandra Hirsh	Jean Reid
Margaret Holtman	Elizabeth Sorenson
Bill Huey	Phyllis Threinen
Kaaren Jacobson	Sondra VanSant
Candice Johnson	Jack Wilson
Jean Kummerow	Adam Yagodka
Sharon Lavoy	

Special notes of thanks go to

Kay Abella, founder and editor of the *TypeWorkS* newsletter. Although *TypeWorkS* is no longer published, we are grateful that the good work of its authors continues through the MBTI® trainers who use these exercises.

Eve E. Delunas for the exercises from *A Potpourri of Group Exercises for Teaching About Type*, presented at the fourth Biennial National Conference on the use of the Myers-Briggs Type Indicator, Palo Alto, CA.

Pat Marr, who developed the cartoons in this book. Pat has granted the right to trainers to copy and use these cartoons for workshop or feedback sessions.

TYPEtype, the official newsletter of the New Zealand Association of Psychological Type.

Introduction

Shape Up Your Program is primarily a book of exercises for those qualified to teach introductory workshops on psychological type.

The impetus for compiling these exercises into a book came from numerous calls CAPT received (and still receives) from MBTI trainers who are looking for new and fresh ideas for presenting basic type concepts in workshops. The exercises herein are easily used by both those newly qualified to use the MBTI tool and those who are more seasoned and experienced trainers.

You will find that the exercises are organized in topical groups, giving the trainer several choices related to a specific aspect of type. The table of contents outlines these topics, giving a variety of training choices. Each exercise includes the following:

- A purpose
- The amount of time needed for the effective presentation of the exercise
- Materials needed
- The process steps for the exercise to be successfully implemented

When giving a workshop, remember that it is always important to include an evaluation process. CAPT is interested in comments from both trainers and participants on how well these exercises work to provide the kind of insight needed for participants to learn about and understand the differences between people.

CAPT is also interested in variations on the exercises and any new exercises that trainers develop to create effective learning environments.

For both evaluation comments and new exercise ideas, send e-mail to ShapeUp@capt.org. We'd appreciate hearing from you. And maybe your training exercise idea will be included in our next book of training and workshop exercises!

Published by the Center for Applications of Psychological Type

Planning a Myers-Briggs Type Indicator Workshop

The first step in planning a workshop is to meet with the client to determine what goals are to be accomplished. Ask questions that help you know what the client wants participants to gain from the workshop experience. Is it building better communication skills, resolving conflict, building better teams, or some other way that knowledge of type can facilitate the effectiveness and productivity of people?

The answers to these questions tell you how much time you need to mount an effective workshop. It is important to have the appropriate amount of time available to accomplish the goals you are trying to meet for the client.

Because most people in your workshop will be learning about type for the first time, a type introduction and verification process will be necessary. In the type community, this is often referred to as a "basic feedback session." It is difficult to accomplish this part of the workshop in less than 2 hours if the type verification process has not already occurred.

The planning phase of mounting a workshop sets the stage for a successful experience, both for the trainer and the participant. Here are some of the most important steps:

- Arrange for the participants to take the Indicator.
- Determine if you want or need any additional reports such as a career or team report.
- Review the scoring results from all of the participants so that you are familiar with their type preferences, clarity of scores, etc.
- Look at the groupings that will work for the kinds of exercises you want to use. This is where you make decisions based on the composition of the group. Unless it is a very large group, you will find it unusual to have adequate type diversification for all of the exercises in this book. (In this case you may want to try a "fishbowl" exercise.)
- Compose a type table that indicates the number of individual types within the group. The type table provides a quick reference for all to see and helps with discussions on some of the strengths and weaknesses related to the type diversity of the group.
- Be familiar with the Ethical Guidelines that are included in this book so that you can answer questions regarding appropriate and inappropriate use of type.
- Write down the goals and objectives for the workshop.
- Make sure that the physical space where you will be holding the workshop is adequate for your needs.
- Develop a design and agenda to meet the workshop goals.
- Determine the kinds of exercises that will support your objectives.
- Gather the materials you will need for the exercises, as well as the type of support publications that you want to distribute to participants.

If the participants are receiving their MBTI results for the first time and an introductory feedback session is indicated, it is important to

- provide an overview of the basic concepts of Jung's theory of psychological types,
- include a type verification process in the workshop design,
- distribute individual reports to participants in such a way as to allow for their privacy in reading those reports, and
- remind participants that individuals have the right to keep their type preferences confidential. (Note: For those who make this choice, the trainer can offer to let them observe rather than to participate. Hopefully, once they see the constructive nature of shared results, they may choose to join other exercises.)

Fishbowl Exercises

Sometimes in a workshop, you will find that there are not enough people of a particular type (or preference) to have an activity that successfully communicates the lesson you are trying to convey. In this case, it is often helpful to use what is known as a "fishbowl" exercise.

A fishbowl exercise is one where a small group of participants is given an assignment that the whole group can observe. In drafting people for such an exercise, it is always best to talk with them ahead of time, or ask for volunteers. Once the volunteers have been selected, then give them the directions for the exercise. Sometimes the observers know what is being illustrated and sometimes they do not.

The physical setup for this type of exercise requires that the participants enacting the assignment sit together in such a way that the entire group can observe what occurs. It is important that everyone be able to see and hear.

Typically, upon completion of the exercise, the whole group debriefs, asks questions, and makes observations.

There are several "fishbowl" exercises in this book.

Published by the Center for Applications of Psychological Type

Tips for Conducting Exercises

If you haven't had a lot of experience in planning and delivering workshops, you will probably find these tips from experts very helpful.

- Create an initial positive experience for all by starting with an exercise where everyone can participate.

- Choose an exercise that will get at the heart of examining the differences in type. When you do, you will tap into the knowledge and experience of those present.

- The simplest task is often the best. The most common mistake for new trainers is to be overly ambitious, often trying to accomplish too much in the time allowed.

- Make sure the exercise can be completed in the time allotted.

- Give clear instructions before you begin the assignment. Let participants know what you are expecting, especially if there is a reporting session at the end of the exercise. It is helpful to distribute the assignment in writing, or write the process steps on flip-chart paper for all to see.

- Clearly specify how subgroups are to be formed and where they are to meet. Allow time for clarifying questions.

- Give a time frame for the exercise and tell the participants or subgroups that you will be giving them periodic time checks. A five minute wrap-up warning is always helpful.

- When having an "end of exercise" reporting session, specify the method for reporting back to the larger group. Give each group the tools that they need to report back. In most cases, a flip chart and markers are adequate. This method will provide both verbal and visual information.

- When several groups are making reports, allow for enough time for each group to complete its reports. Processing similarities and differences can take more time than you might have planned. Before you begin the reporting session, check your watch and divide the allotted time by the number of reports to be given. Tell the groups ahead of time that you are going to keep track of time.

- It is the instructor's role to point out the teaching points when group reports are being made. Ask members questions, when appropriate, such as the following:
    - What observations do you have about the group's process?
    - How did you feel while you were participating in the exercise?
    - What differences have you noticed between the groups?
    - Do you think those differences relate to type?

- The "aha" experience is more likely to occur if the participants generate the ideas themselves.

- Process time is the most important time for learning. As a rule, it should involve twice as much time as the exercise itself.

Type-Tuning Your Presentations

Public speaking is one of the top things that people fear the most. One participant in a presentation skills class was overheard to say, "I'd rather die than give a speech."

You may agree with him, or you may thrive on the challenge of speaking to groups. Either way, you've undoubtedly noticed that presentations are an organizational fact of life. Clearly, presentation competence is a business and career tool worth sharpening.

Start by giving yourself an edge in making presentations: take type preferences into account. Since you don't usually know what types will be in the audience, the best strategy is to consider the information needs of all type preferences. As a guideline, think 4x4 when preparing presentation content and delivery. This will keep you focused on the presentation preferences of the 4 attitudes and the 4 functions.

4 Attitudes
The attitudes influence the delivery—*how* people like to have information presented.

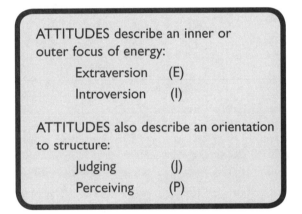

ATTITUDES describe an inner or outer focus of energy:

Extraversion   (E)
Introversion   (I)

ATTITUDES also describe an orientation to structure:

Judging   (J)
Perceiving   (P)

4 Functions
The functions influence the content—*what* information people want included.

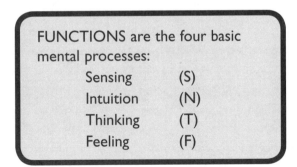

FUNCTIONS are the four basic mental processes:

Sensing   (S)
Intuition   (N)
Thinking   (T)
Feeling   (F)

Published by the Center for Applications of Psychological Type

For the Extraverts

- Convey energy and enthusiasm about the topic.
- Give implications for action.
- Allow time for participation and discussion.

For the Introverts

- Provide written materials ahead—especially if you want discussion or decisions immediately.
- Pause when asking for response—20 seconds is effective.
- Be prepared to draw out some individuals with specific questions.

For the Sensing Types

- Include specifics, facts, and details.
- Show why it is realistic, makes sense.
- Include real life applications and examples of where this has worked before.

For the Intuitive Types

- Give an overview of your presentation at the beginning; put it in context.
- Mention several possibilities.
- Talk about cutting edge happenings.

For the Thinking Types

- List all the costs and benefits, pros and cons.
- Structure your information logically.
- State any abstract principles or theories involved.
- Be succinct.

For the Feeling Types

- Be friendly, collaborative.
- Show the impact on people, especially why it is important to the individuals involved.
- Tell who supports the idea.
- Express appreciation for others' contributions.

For the Judging Types

- Start and end on time; state at the beginning how long you will speak.
- Present information in a structured framework.
- Be organized in using audiovisual support materials; have a practice session.

For the Perceiving Types

- Respond to questions or issues arising during the presentation.
- Offer the presentation as an opportunity to explore options or gather data.
- Use process words: completing, discussing, examining.

> If this 4x4 list looks like a lot to keep in mind, remember that your presentation style usually reflects your own preferences; half these suggestions will come naturally to you. So for the maximum impact, focus on the hints for your nonpreferred functions and attitudes.

Developed by Sue Dutton. (Reprinted from *TypeWorks* with permission.)

MBTI Code of Ethics

The following ethical guidelines were excerpted from the Myers & Briggs Foundation website (www. myersbriggs.org). These guidelines were compiled from various sources, and refined and organized to provide MBTI facilitators with the most accurate and current information for ethically administering and providing feedback for the MBTI instrument.

General Guidelines

(1) Identify type theory as the work of C. G. Jung and the MBTI instrument as the work of Isabel Briggs Myers and Katharine C. Briggs.

(2) Present psychological type as **describing healthy personality differences,** not psychological disorders or fixed traits.

(3) Be adamant that **all types are valuable;** no type is better, healthier, or more desirable in any way.

(4) Describe preference and types in **nonjudgmental terms** at all times; be aware of how your own type biases may influence your words.

(5) Present type preferences as **tendencies, preferences, or inclinations,** rather than absolutes.

(6) Stress that type **does not imply excellence, competence, or natural ability,** only what is *preferred.*

(7) Never imply that all people of a certain type behave in the same way; type should **not be used to put people in rigid categories.**

(8) Explain how people **sometimes act in ways contrary to their preferences** because of pressure from family, relationships, job environment, or culture. Consistent forced use of nonpreferred preferences can cause stress.

(9) When describing preferences, **distinguish between what has been shown by research and what are anecdotes to illustrate type.**

Ethics for Administering the Myers-Briggs Type Indicator Instrument

(1) Tell respondents that taking the Indicator is **always voluntary** and offer the opportunity not to participate.

(2) Insist that Indicator results **never be used to label,** evaluate, or limit the respondent in any way.

(3) Ensure that type results are **confidential** and not given to anyone besides the respondent without permission.

(4) Inform respondents of the purpose of taking the instrument and how results will be used.

(5) Tell respondents the Indicator is **not a test,** since there are no right or wrong answers.

(6) If the instrument is given for research purposes, sharing the results with respondents is not required but highly recommended.

(7) **Do not take specific questions** from the Indicator to get a "quick reading" on a particular preference pair.

(8) Administer and score the Indicator in accordance with the guidelines in the most current edition of the *MBTI® Manual.*

Published by the Center for Applications of Psychological Type

Ethical Feedback of MBTI Results

(1) Give results directly to the respondent as part of an active discussion with a qualified administrator. Never deliver results in impersonal ways such as through e-mail or mail.

(2) Present type results as a **working hypothesis,** a starting point for further exploration.

(3) Make it clear that **the respondent is the expert;** the only person who can verify which type fits best.

(4) Allow respondents to **self-assess their preferences** based on the introduction to type, prior to giving results of the Indicator.

(5) Do not become defensive if the respondent disagrees with the report results. **Help the respondent explore his or her hesitations** and identify a comfortable best-fit type.

(6) Provide descriptions of all sixteen types to help determine best-fit type. Recommend additional materials for further study.

(7) Do not counsel a person toward or away from a particular career, relationship, or activity based solely upon type information; type does not explain everything.

(8) Make it clear that the preference clarity indexes in the results do not imply excellence, competence, or maturity. They reflect only consistency in choosing one preference over another.

(9) Make sure the respondent sees the **feedback session as the beginning of the process.** Knowing one's type is not a one-time understanding, but a guide to ongoing growth and development toward an individual's potential.

Ethics for Professional Qualifications

(1) Even those who are qualified to purchase the Indicator by their educations will want to study materials specifically about the MBTI instrument so they can offer comprehensive background and guidance to a respondent. The MBTI instrument is different from other instruments. Without in-depth understanding, the feedback could be shallow or inaccurate. Perhaps most important, qualified users who do not seek additional training may miss opportunities to use the full richness of the theory.

(2) Many qualified users update their knowledge and expertise regularly with continuing education activities such as conferences and workshops.

Interpreting MBTI Results

(1) The administrator must use terms and descriptors that are nonjudgmental and describe type attributes as tendencies, preferences, or inclinations rather than as absolutes. Biased terms may slant interpretation or send messages that a particular preference is "good" or "not desirable."

(2) The administrator should be careful not to over-generalize or over-simplify results and imply that all people of a certain type behave the same way.

(3) One should not state or imply that type explains everything. Type does not reflect an individual's ability, intelligence, likelihood of success, emotions, or normalcy. Type is one important component of the complex human personality.

(4) The administrator should not impose the results on the respondent or become defensive if the respondent disagrees with the reported results or does not believe they are accurate. One should explore the perceived differences and help respondents to be comfortable with themselves.

(5) Administrators need to be aware of, and sensitive to, their own type biases and exert every effort to present feedback in an objective way.

(6) It is unethical and in many cases illegal to require job applicants to take the Indicator if the results will be used to screen out applicants. The administrator should not counsel a person to, or away from, a particular career, personal relationship, or activity based solely upon type information.

(7) Administrators should accurately represent their competence and experience to clients.

(8) Administrators should continually upgrade their knowledge of the Indicator and advances in the understanding and application of type through education (workshops, seminars, conferences), reading, or other means.

(9) Administrators should provide respondents with materials that describe all 16 types.

Published by the Center for Applications of Psychological Type

Frequently Asked Questions

Q: A refresher on the dominant and inferior: which is which?

A: The two middle letters in any MBTI type indicate the preferred functions of that type. One is the dominant or most preferred function; the other is the auxiliary or second most preferred function.

The types whose dominant function is Thinking are ESTJ, ENTJ, ISTP, and INTP. The types with Feeling as their dominant function are ESFJ, ENFJ, ISFP, and INFP.

The types whose dominant function is Sensing are ESTP, ESFP, ISTJ, and ISFJ. The types with Intuition as their dominant function are ENTP, ENFP, INTJ, and INFJ.

The inferior function of any type is the fourth or least used function. It does not even appear in the type letters, since it is the opposite of the dominant function and operates largely in the unconscious. So the inferior function for types with dominant Thinking is Feeling and the inferior function for types with dominant Feeling is Thinking. For types with dominant Sensing the inferior is Intuition, while the inferior function for types with dominant Intuition is Sensing.

The inferior is used in the opposite world from the dominant. So, for example, an ENTJ's dominant T is used in the external world; the inferior F is used in the internal world. An ENTJ's inferior would then be called introverted Feeling.

Under stress, first the dominant function is used more and more until it becomes distorted. Then, under continued stress, the inferior function starts to take over. It usually appears as a negative version of that same function when it is dominant. So for example, dominant Feeling is a strong unconscious use of Feeling while inferior Feeling is a less effective unconscious or "primitive" version of the Feeling function.

Q: Why is extravert spelled with an "a" in MBTI materials instead of the more usual spelling with an "o"?

A: In the official translation of Jung's *Psychological Types,* the spelling is *extravert.* In the sixth edition of Robert Campbell's *Psychiatric Dictionary, extraversion* is used. In my Webster's *New World Dictionary,* I find *extrovert* with the derivation "from the Latin *extra* (outside) and *vertere* (to turn)." I also find *introvert* with the derivation "from the Latin *intro* (within) and *vertere* (to turn)."

I have always used extraversion because Isabel Myers used it, Jung used it, and because I used to teach Latin and extraversion is more faithful to the Latin root *extra.*

Years ago when I taught Latin and studied linguistics, I vaguely remember the term *ultracorrection.* It referred to a time in the development of English when scholars "neatened it up" and made it more logical. Perhaps extroversion is the result of ultracorrection.

In summary, extraversion is the spelling used for work by C. G. Jung and work derived from Jung. It is also faithful to its Latin roots.

(Mary McCaulley)

Q: Did Carl Jung ever know about the Myers-Briggs Type Indicator?

A: In the 1920s and 1930s, Katharine Briggs corresponded sporadically with Jung about his type theory and other matters. In 1937, Katharine met Jung when he lectured at Yale, but the type indicator was not yet developed. She told him she had been working on a theory of type but had burned her notes after reading Jung's book *Psychological Types* and realizing that his ideas encompassed hers. Jung said she should not have destroyed her work because it might have made a real contribution to type psychology. Jung later had copies of his seminar notes sent to Katharine.

In 1950, Katharine's daughter, Isabel Briggs Myers, wrote to Jung asking to visit him on an upcoming trip to Europe. She enclosed a three-page description of the MBTI instrument and a sample of Form C. The seventy-five-year-old Jung replied with regret that a bad bout of gastric flu plus an upcoming long holiday would not allow him to meet with her.

He thanked her for the "interesting questionnaire and equally interesting description of your results." He added, "As you have given the matter a great deal of thought I think you have done so much in this direction that I'm hardly capable of criticizing it or even knowing it better ... But I should say that for any future development of the Type-Theory your Type-Indicator will prove to be of great help."
(TypeWorkS)

Q: What does it mean if my score is near the middle?

A: The answer is the same for any preference. Let's use T–F as an example. If your T–F score is near the middle, it means you pretty much split your votes between Thinking choices and Feeling choices.

Does that mean that I am an expert in using Thinking and an expert in using Feeling? That I have good type development and I can do everything?

Unfortunately, that is rarely true. When a preference score is near the middle, the most important issue is that the person is saying, "I am not clear about my type. I don't know if I am an (for example) ESFJ or ESTJ." Thus the important issue is which type category fits best, rather than what the strength of the scores mean. "There are a number of reasons a person might not be clear about a preference. It's worth our taking time to talk about it, because the information from the MBTI instrument is more valuable if you agree that one of the types is a good fit for you." However, it is not a weakness of character to be unclear about a preference. Discovering one's type is a developmental process, and can take time.
(Mary McCaulley)

Q: How does a person get to be a type?

A: Jung believed that we are born with a predisposition for one type. Environmental factors are important, however, because they can foster type development or get in its way. One of the four mental processes (S, N, T, or F) and one attitude (E or I) are your natural bent, according to Jung, and these natural processes make up the heart of type.
(Gordon Lawrence)

Q: Doesn't type fence you in?

A: Not if you understand it. An understanding of type frees you in several ways. It gives you confidence in your own direction of development: the areas in which you can become excellent with the most ease and pleasure. It can also reduce the guilt many people feel at not being able to do everything in life equally well. As Isabel Myers put it, "For most people, really understanding their own type in particular, and other people's types in general, is a releasing experience rather than a restricting one. It sets one free to recognize one's own natural bent and to trust one's own potential for growth and excellence, with no obligation to copy anyone else, however admirable that person may be in his or her own different way." Finally, acknowledging your own preferences opens the possibility of finding constructive values instead of conflicts in the differences you encounter with someone whose preferences are opposite yours.

(Gordon Lawrence)

Q: Can you change your type?

A: Scores on the MBTI instrument can be changed depending on how you answer the questions. Score changes can result in a report of a different type. Jung seemed to believe that each person has a true type that he or she may not yet have discovered. The true type does not change, although it may seem to, as one focuses on developing different mental processes at different stages of one's life. Behaviors can change, of course, but their roots remain the same.

However, there are many reasons you might take the MBTI instrument two different times and come out different types. You might still be discovering your preferences, and trying them on for size. Or you might be working especially hard to develop one of the mental processes, so that you report it on the MBTI instrument with stronger than usual emphasis. Or, you might take the instrument one time as your "job self," responding as you see yourself acting on the job, and you might take it another time as your "home self," responding as you see yourself in your home environment. If your type differs between two reports, this fact may lead to interesting information about yourself. As you cast your thoughts back to your frame of mind when you were answering the questions, consider how it may have affected your reporting of yourself and whether it reflects your true type.

(Gordon Lawrence)

Q: What's the best type to be?

A: For you, the type you really are. Jung's theory says your best satisfactions in life will be those that come through the strengths of your type.

(Gordon Lawrence)

Q: Is everyone of the same type alike?

A: No. There are many individual differences within each type, because many things influence personality besides type. Some people are at a higher level of type development than others. Even in people of the same type who are well-developed, there are big differences. Take an ESFJ for example. You would expect all the ESFJs to share a wish for people around them to be happy, and would work to achieve harmony. Some ESFJs might be interested in education and be teachers; others might become family doctors and others salespersons. Still others might find their way of helping in volunteer work, or in being a good parent. All these activities offer effective ways of using Feeling in the outer world, as extraverted Feeling types are predicted to do.

(Gordon Lawrence)

Q: Can I use the MBTI tool for hiring purposes?

A: Hiring decisions need to go beyond looking for more people in the frequent types. There are not now, and I doubt there ever will be, data to say that any type will succeed or fail in any occupation. Unless you can prove that MBTI scores relate specifically to performance in a specific job, it would be unethical and unwise to hire on the basis of the MBTI instrument. After the hiring process the instrument can be used (with the employee's consent) as part of teamwork or management development programs. In this setting, there is time for deeper understanding of type and a greater appreciation of one's own gifts, and seeing how "constructive use of differences" leads to cooperation.

(Mary McCaulley)

Q: How many of my type are there in the country?

A: We are not exactly sure how many, but we do have some estimates. CAPT publishes a handout titled *Estimated Frequencies of the Types in the United States Population*. A sample of this handout can be viewed at www.capt.org.

Q: Does a country or culture have a type? What types predominate in a country or culture?

A: At this point there is no good answer to these questions. Part of the problem is in obtaining good translations and samples from the different cultures. The MBTI instrument has been translated into many languages, but we don't have stratified random samples from the countries. We assume that every culture will have citizens from all sixteen MBTI types, and so far research is confirming this assumption. However, the behaviors associated with a preference may vary from one culture to another. For example, an extraverted Japanese male may behave very differently from an extraverted Italian male because of cultural influences. We are also finding that certain patterns transcend cultural differences (e.g., TJ types are found frequently among managers in all countries.) However, we do not yet have sufficient data to say whether cultures will differ in the pattern of distribution of the sixteen types.

(Mary McCaulley)

Published by the Center for Applications of Psychological Type

Getting Started

How to Market Your MBTI Program

Feedback can be given to almost any group that has an interest and desire for personal development and self-knowledge. When you are building a consulting business it is assumed that you would integrate the MBTI training into your own area of expertise (e.g., career counseling, team enhancement, leadership coaching, organizational development).

How do you get started if you do not already have an established base of clients? Network, network, network!

Some Tips on Networking

- Let your friends, colleagues, and family members know of your interest in conducting MBTI training as part of your consulting/training business.
- Contact your local American Society for Training and Development (ASTD) chapter and participate in the meetings.
- Offer to provide an MBTI program for an ASTD meeting so members can see what you have to offer.
- Offer to speak at other organizational meetings such as the Society for Human Resource Managers (SHRM), trade organizations, civic groups, religious, and education groups.
- Participate in local and national meetings and conferences.
- Prepare a research or applications paper to present at a regional or national conference.
- Write an article for a newsletter outlining the benefits of using the MBTI instrument.
- Participate in meetings, seminars, and conferences for your particular area of expertise.
- Contact your local high school, community college, or university to meet with the career resource center or other interested departments. Let them know what you can do for them.

Keeping Current

Networking is essential but it is not enough. Consultants must stay abreast of the latest findings in their specialized field. To do this you should:

- Read current books, articles, and other publications related to your specific area of interest.
- Attend conferences.
- Attend professional training programs.
- Subscribe to newsletters or other publications in your area of interest.

Presentation Skills

The last tip would be to evaluate your presentation skills and style. It is not always what you say, but how you say it and how you deliver it. If you are rusty or do not know how someone else would assess your ability to speak and interact in front of a group, ask a friend or colleague for feedback. Most cities have a Toastmasters group, speakers bureau, or other similar group to contact for assistance. Practice with friends or family. Audio and/or video tape a sample presentation. Critique yourself and also ask others to critique your presentation.

Practice presenting a program to a church group, nonprofit, or civic group free of charge (or charge just enough to cover expenses). Bring along a trusted colleague who can and will give you feedback, or hand out an evaluation at the conclusion of the program as a way of getting feedback.

There is no substitute for knowledge and expertise. Building on the foundation of knowledge takes networking skills, presentation skills, and a constant awareness of what is new in your field.

Published by the Center for Applications of Psychological Type

Valuing Differences

Purpose: To demonstrate differences between Extraversion and Introversion and learn to value the differences.

Time: 20 to 30 minutes

Materials: Flip-chart paper and markers.

Process: (1) Divide larger group into E and I groups.

(2) Post on flip-chart paper the following questions for each group to answer.
- *What do you really admire about the other group?*
- *What baffles you about the other group?*
- *What question(s) do you have for the other group?*

(3) Ask each group to write down their responses on a large piece of newsprint and choose a person from the group to report to the larger group. Allow time to process the responses from each group.

It's not that I change my mind.
It's that everyone insists I answer "right
now." So I do—and then when I know
what I mean—I tell them.

LaVonne Neff, *One of a Kind*

Conversation Sticks

Purpose: To demonstrate differences between Extraversion/Introversion preferences.

Time: 10 minutes

Materials: Enough small objects that can be easily counted, such as popsicle sticks, pencils, poker chips, cardboard strips, etc., to give 3 or 4 to each person.

Process: (1) Give 3 or 4 countable objects to each person. Divide into teams of 5 to 7 members to discuss a topic of interest to the participants. Be sure that each team includes both Es and Is. Each time a participant talks, they put their "counter" in the middle. When all of their counters are gone, they cannot talk again until everyone has used all of their counters, the counters are redistributed, and the process starts again. Be sure to let Introverts know that they can summarize what others have said as part of their turn if they do not want to contribute new ideas.

(2) After 5 minutes, stop the discussion and talk about the process.

- Who ran out of sticks first?
- How did they feel when they ran out of sticks?
- Did the Introverts feel uncomfortable, like they were being forced to talk?
- Did the Introverts find themselves talking more because it was expected?
- Who talked the longest?

Developed by Elizabeth Murphy.

Published by the Center for Applications of Psychological Type

Numbers Game

Purpose: Demonstrate E–I differences.

Time: 10 to 20 minutes depending on the size of the group

Materials: A note card for each participant with a number on it from 1 to 5.

Process: (1) BEFORE discussing E–I, give each participant a note card with a number on it.

(2) Tell everyone to stand up and form groups of people whose numbers total 12 (or as close to 12 as possible).

(3) After groups seem to have formed, ask the participants to sit back down and tell what they observed about how people got into groups. It is usually fairly evident that the Es shout out their need while the Is walk around and look at other cards or approach others one-on-one. (You may also observe J–P behavior during this exercise that you can refer to later during your discussion of J–P.)

If you don't know what an Extravert is thinking,
you haven't been listening. If you don't know
what an Introvert is thinking, you haven't asked.

Isabel Briggs Myers

Developed by Candice Johnson.

Demonstrating Preferences

Purpose: To demonstrate differences in the Sensing–Intuition preferences.

Time: 15 minutes

Materials: Flip-chart paper, markers, and a leaf. Sometimes people will want to go outside and look at leaves.

Process: (1) Divide group into S and N groups. Separate the groups as much as possible (i.e., opposite corners of the room).

(2) Ask the groups to write a few words or sentences about a leaf. Allow some time for discussion. Ask them as a group to write down their answers on the flip-chart paper.

(3) Bring the groups back together and ask the Ss to report first. They will tend to report a lot of sensory impressions. They also tend to start with the object and stay with it. Any associations they mention will most likely be connected to real memories and concrete associations. Lead a discussion on the words or phrases focusing on whether the S or N function was revealed.

(4) Next ask the Ns to report. They may start with the object but it then becomes a leaping off point. They will mention a few facts that they then use to take off from and form associations. They may list associations such as "leaves of grass," "Leif Eriksson," "table leaves," etc. They may add details about these associations. Process the group discussion bringing out the differences.

Variations: (A) Ask each group to write a few words or sentences about a styrofoam cup.

(B) Ask each group to write a few words, phrases, or sentences about a poster of a painting that you display. (Salvador Dalí's paintings generate interesting discussions.)

(C) If it is a small group, have them work individually. Tell them their task is "to write" and the topic is "leaf." (If you say "leaf" rather than "a leaf," you may have an N come up with Leif Eriksson!)

Examples of Answers to the Describe-a-Leaf Exercise

Sensing	Intuitive	Intuitive (cont'd.)
fall	grows	make good compost
crunchy	photosynthesis	decorative
smell	color texture	tea
colorful	fall from trees	smoke
slippery when wet	vary in shape	drink
rake them	indicate wind	eat
pile them	if brown—dead	dip
burn them	indicate health of plant	chew
life cycle	geographically different	wear
produce oxygen	can make a bed	functional aesthetic
food	they crunch	symbol
shade	can play in them	pages of a book
allergies	smell good when they burn	good luck
	slippery when wet	table expansion
		gold leaf

NOTE: In this type of exercise, the Sensing group's list is often shorter than that of the Intuitives. Intuitives tend to enjoy the brain-storming process. Also, observe the outward attitude of Judging and Perceiving. The SJs' list will be concise and to the point, whereas NPs may run out of time before they run out of ideas.

Civilization is the encouragement of differences.

Mahatma Gandhi

Experiencing Sensing and Intuition

This exercise experientially demonstrates the S–N preference pair after participants are introduced to type and process their own type descriptions.

Purpose: To demonstrate the effect of the S and N preferences on behavior.

Time: 30 minutes

Materials: You need two identical sets of Tinker Toys, Legos, or similar building materials and copies of the observation sheets shown on the following pages.

Process: (1) Announce that two groups (4 or 5 volunteers each) will do the same task in turn while others observe. Ask for volunteers who are fairly clear they have an S preference. A mixture of Extraverts and Introverts is helpful.

(2) Give this Sensing group one set of building materials with instructions to "together build a structure" in five minutes. They can talk with each other while building.

(3) Before building begins, hand out copies of the "Sensing Observation Worksheet" (see page 22) to *other* program participants for their observations. Tell observers not to talk to the builders.

(4) When the sensing types' five-minute building time is up, leave their structure in place. Do not discuss observations at this time.

(5) Repeat Steps 1 to 4 with an Intuitive group, using the second set of building materials and "Intuition Observation Worksheet" (see page 23) for observers.

(6) On a piece of flip-chart paper with a line down the middle, write S above one column and N above the other. Ask for observations on both the product and the process, placing comments in either column as appropriate. Keep reminding the group they are looking for observations on both the product and the process of creating it. They are to refer to their observation sheets. This step takes about 10 minutes.

> **Note:** Observers find it helpful when the facilitator has previously discussed concrete examples of the possible behaviors on the observation sheets, particularly those on the Intuitive list as these are often more difficult to observe.

Developed by Waite Maclin. (Reprinted with permission from *TypeWorkS.*)

Published by the Center for Applications of Psychological Type

Sensing Observation Worksheet

Observe participants as they work on the structure. How do they communicate, what do they communicate, what methods do they use to create the structure, what do they intend it to be, and what is the final product? Jot down anything you observe.

> **Please do not say anything to the participants during the exercise.**

Possible Sensing behaviors you may observe:
- Stating the facts
- Being realistic
- Organizing; attention to detail
- Finding out exactly what the situation is and what is being done about it
- Using the five senses
- Doing things, trying things (e.g., move pieces around)

Observations

_____

_____

_____

_____

_____

_____

_____

_____

_____

_____

_____

_____

_____

Intuition Observation Worksheet

Observe participants as they work on the structure. How do they communicate, what do they communicate, what methods do they use to create the structure, what do they intend it to be, and what is the final product? Jot down anything you observe.

> **Please do not say anything to the participants during the exercise.**

Possible Intuitive behaviors you may observe:
- Identifying all the possibilities
- Considering all the ways the situation might be changed
- Looking for possibilities for different approaches the group may take
- Having hunches
- Thinking (and speaking) globally or in regard to "The Big Picture"
- Talking about what might be done rather than actually doing it

Observations

_____

_____

_____

_____

_____

_____

_____

_____

_____

_____

_____

_____

Published by the Center for Applications of Psychological Type

Group Story

Purpose: To demonstrate differences between Sensing and Intuitive types.

Time: 15 to 20 minutes

Materials: One collage of tools, paper for participants to write on, writing utensils, word lists for each participant (see page 25). NOTE: The instructor will need to create the collage ahead of time.

Process: (1) BEFORE introducing the S–N preferences, use the collage to divide the group into approximate S and N groups. Show the participants the collage which is made up of various kinds of tools. Ask them to look at the collage for 2 minutes.

(2) Then cover the collage and ask the participants to write down what they saw. Tell the participants that this is NOT a contest to see who can write down the most.

(3) After about half a minute, ask each participant to read what she/he has written. Then ask the group to divide themselves into 2 groups based on what they have heard. Usually it is pretty clear that some people have given specific answers (they have listed the various tools) and some people have given more general answers (such as "tools"). Have the participants move and sit with those who gave similar answers.

(4) Give a copy of the list of words to each participant. Ask each group to take 5 minutes to write a group story using as many of the words on the list as possible. (You may notice J–P differences as they are completing this exercise and may want to refer back to the differences when discussing J–P).

(5) Have each group read its story out loud. Usually the difference is striking, both in content and in structure. Some word usage is quite predictable; for example, every S group I have ever had do this exercise has used the word *tractor*. No S group has ever used the word *azure*, yet every N group has used the word *azure*!

Developed by Candice Johnson.

Word List

azure	glide	red
balloon	glow	restful
black	green	road
blue	grow	run
bright	hilly	soak
brilliant	home	solitude
calm	horse	stand
clip	intimidate	sun
cloud	lake	thunder
content	meander	tractor
corner	mirror	tree
crane	motion	twenty
crisp	orange	willow
deer	paper	wind
dream	pasture	window
fence	power	wispy
fly	quaint	
furry	quiet	
gentle	rain	

Published by the Center for Applications of Psychological Type

Tea Bag Exercise

Purpose: To provide experiential evidence of the differences between Introverted Sensing and Extraverted Sensing and Introverted Intuition and Extraverted Intuition.

Time: About 45 minutes

Materials: Flip-chart paper and markers.

Process: (1) Set up 4 flip charts in the corners of the room. Charts should be labeled Introverted Sensing, Extraverted Sensing, Introverted Intuition, Extraverted Intuition. Each chart may also be labeled with the four types having that function-attitude as a dominant or auxiliary.

(2) Ask each participant to go to the appropriate chart for the perceiving function of his or her type. If some people are undecided about their type, have them choose the perceiving functions they believe best describe the ways they gather information. Announce that each group will be given an object. The group is to talk about the object and then record their discussion points on the flip chart.

(3) After removing any identifying labels from four tea bags, give one to each group. Allow 10 minutes for the small group discussion. If any participants feel they are not in the right groups, as the discussion goes on, they are free to move to another group.

(4) Ask each group to report in this order; Extraverted Sensing, Introverted Sensing, Extraverted Intuition, Introverted Intuition. As each group reports, point out similarities and differences in what was discussed and recorded, particularly in the extraverted and introverted forms of the same function.

S_e Usually the Extraverted Sensing group reports on the actual physical description of the tea bag—size, and how it looks, feels, smells, or tastes.

S_i The Introverted Sensing group tends to connect the tea bag with past experiences with tea, for example, tea as a comfort when one is not feeling well or tea parties as a child.

Developed by Leona Haas. (Reprinted with permission from *TypeWorkS*.)

N$_e$ Typically the Extraverted Intuition group literally has a "brainstorm" and their report shows many possible uses of the tea bag, often organized into patterns of use as well.

N$_i$ The Introverted Intuition group, in contrast, will often present pages and pages of associations to the tea bag. But the associations are so personal and seemingly tangential that observers are often baffled by the connection to the tea bag.

An interesting question to ask each group is, "Where is your tea bag now?" The Extraverted Sensing group usually has it in hand, can show it to the whole group, or has attached it to the chart. The Introverted Sensing tea bag may or may not be in evidence. Almost always both N groups have lost track of the actual tea bag. For them it was only a starting point and the actual object is not important.

You should also point out the wide diversity of results, noting that all groups had exactly the same directions and the same object.

Published by the Center for Applications of Psychological Type

Decision Making

Purpose: To allow participants to experience the Zig-Zag method of problem solving.

Time: 40 to 60 minutes

Materials: Timer

Process: (1) Divide into groups and, if possible, make sure each group has one person representing each dominant preference. Have the groups decide on a problem they wish to solve; for example, "Is now a good time for Gary to start his furniture refinishing business?"

(2) Explain that you are going to try to even out the amount of time spent on each of the phases of the decision-making process. Encourage the participants to identify each person's dominant in their group and to agree to allow those persons to lead the part of the activity that revolves around their dominant function.

(3) Set the timer for 6 minutes and ask the groups to engage in only an S kind of discussion for that time. Monitor each group, if possible, to keep them on track—no N, T, or F discussions allowed for these 6 minutes! When time is up, move on to N, then T, then F, allowing 6 minutes of each, following the Zig-Zag model.

(4) Debrief, discussing the process. Participants are often amazed how slowly time seemed to go for some of the processes and how quickly for others!

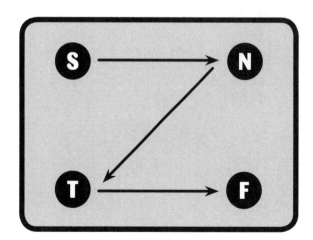

Developed by Candice Johnson.

Balanced Hiring Decisions

Purpose: To have participants practice and observe an interview and a hiring decision using a balance of Sensing, Intuition, Thinking, and Feeling.

Time: About 45 minutes

Materials: A handout or list for each participant of Sensing probes and Intuitive probes and a flip chart.

Process: (1) Ask for volunteers for a "fishbowl" role-play of a job interview. Position the interviewer and candidate in the center of the space with other participants around them.

(2) Provide background information about the job. If this is a behavioral interview, provide appropriate structured questions. Pass out a list of Sensing probes and Intuitive probes and encourage role-players to use a mixture of the two, in order to collect the most complete information. You may also choose to have the class generate the two lists.

(3) Instruct the observers to help you keep track of how many Sensing probes and how many Intuitive probes are used.

(4) During the 10- to 15-minute interview, make check marks on a flip chart for each Sensing probe and each Intuitive probe used.

(5) When the interview is over, explore the balance between the two types of probes and the effect on the information gained in the interview. Point out any information missed because of a lack of either Sensing or Intuitive probes.

(6) Now ask all the participants whether they would hire this candidate and why. Point out which reasons seem based on Thinking criteria and which on Feeling criteria. Point out how both sets of criteria need to be taken into account to make the best hiring decision.

(7) If appropriate, point out where the decision is made harder because of information not gathered in the interview.

Developed by Margaret Holtman. (Reprinted with permission from *TypeWorkS*.)

Published by the Center for Applications of Psychological Type

Sensing probes:

How much?

How many?

How often?

Who?

Where?

When?

What kind?

Intuitive probes:

Tell me more.

What else should I know?

Why do you say that?

For example . . . ?

Echoing the words of the candidate.

Experience a Peanut

Purpose: This activity helps people distinguish between the mental processes of perception (Sensing and Intuition) and judgment (Thinking and Feeling).

Time: 20 to 30 minutes

Materials: Bag of peanuts (or apples, mints, popcorn), writing paper.

Process: (1) Divide the group into pairs with one partner being a recorder. Both talk, one writes. The recorder should mark off four sections on a sheet of note paper. Label one section "Sensing," one "Intuition," one "Feeling," and one "Thinking." Make notes in each section, as indicated below, starting with Sensing.

(2) Both persons eat a peanut, paying attention to one process at a time. Take 3 or 4 minutes for each process.

(3) Ask participants to do the following:

• As you encounter the peanut, list your sense impressions of the peanut and its parts—noting colors, shapes, textures, tastes, muscular movements, and tensions. List facts only.

• List the intuitions that come to you during the experience. Memories and associations: Who or what do peanuts make you think of? Can you recall other ways of enjoying peanuts? Do you recall peanuts in stories, songs, etc? Do you find yourself speculating about this particular peanut?

• List your feelings:
  ○ How you felt about trying this experiment.
  ○ How you felt about eating the peanut you chose.

• Can you think about peanuts?
  ○ Did your sense impressions or your intuitions lead you to make any logical conclusions about this peanut? About peanuts in general?

(4) As a group, process the following kinds of questions:
• How do your Sensing data differ from your Intuition data?
• Do those differences help you to understand why people who prefer Sensing are basically different from people who prefer Intuition?
• How do your Feeling judgments differ from your Thinking judgments?
• Do those differences help you understand the basic differences between people who prefer to make Feeling judgments and those who prefer Thinking judgments?

Developed by Gordon Lawrence. (Adapted from *People Types and Tiger Stripes*. Used with permission.)

Published by the Center for Applications of Psychological Type

Whose Ideal?

Purpose: To demonstrate the differing contributions of people with Feeling and Thinking preferences in designing a system.

Time: 35 to 45 minutes

Materials: Flip-chart paper and markers.

Process: (1) Introduce the principle of brainstorming; participants list their ideas but do not discuss them, although definitions or explanations may be requested by other participants.

(2) Divide the class into groups whose preference is Thinking or Feeling. Limit size of groups to 6 to 8 members.

(3) Ask the groups to "brainstorm and list on a flip chart the critical elements of an ideal educational system." Allow about 10 to 15 minutes. You may note that the Thinking groups are having a hard time NOT debating. Do not interfere but note these examples for the discussion.

(4) Have each group present its flip chart briefly; then ask for comments on the differences between the results of the Thinking and Feeling groups. The main differences that will be apparent are as follows:
- People preferring Thinking list what is needed structurally and organizationally.
- People preferring Feeling list all the ingredients that make people feel wanted, needed, appreciated, cared for, or equal.
- People preferring Thinking tend to list items in a concise orderly manner, often numbered.
- People with a Feeling preference create a more random list, scattered over the flip chart. This is often the result of this group wanting to be sure everyone's ideas are included.

You may also ask for comments about the difference in the brainstorming process between the Feeling and Thinking groups.

(5) Ask people to consider what would happen if either group moved ahead without the input of the other. Summarize by pointing out how both perspectives are needed to reach an ideal.

Developed by C. Waite Maclin. (Reprinted with permission from *TypeWorkS*.)

Variations: (A) The topic can be altered to more closely fit the group you are working with. For example, you could ask about the critical elements of an ideal political system or ideal health care system.

(B) You can have a person of Feeling preference observe the Thinking group and vice versa. These people can then comment during the discussion, based on their preference being opposite that of the groups they observed.

Published by the Center for Applications of Psychological Type

The T–F Decision

Purpose: To distinguish Thinking–Feeling differences.

Time: 10 to 20 minutes

Materials: None

Process: (1) As facilitator, you role play a Feeling type (F) talking to a Thinking type (T) about a sensitive issue.

First role play the F: "So and so is in my class. She has a child with leukemia and has had a hard time this semester. She took the tests several times and she tried hard, but she still failed them. I want to pass her anyway, not a high grade but passing. She tried hard, but she just has so much else going on. She seems to be able to talk about the information but can't produce on paper."

Then role play the T: "She has already been given a chance to take the tests several times. There's no way we can make an exception for her. We have to be up front about it. It's not fair to the others in the class to pass her. It is certainly unfortunate what she is having to go through, but we can't make exceptions."

(2) Ask the participants, "Who's right? Whom do you agree with?"
- Fs will usually agree with the F point of view.
- Ts usually agree with the T point of view. If there are Fs who agree with the T side and vice versa, it is interesting to explore why.

Variation: Ask the group what they would do if one of their employees was stealing from the cash register. The employee is a single parent with two small children who has been receiving federal assistance because of low income.
- Ts may start talking prosecution.
- Fs may want to pay the employee more.

Developed by Eve Delunas.

Problem Solving

Purpose: To demonstrate different approaches of Thinking–Feeling in problem solving.

Time: 20 to 30 minutes

Materials: None

Process: (1) Divide the group into groups whose preference is Thinking and those whose preference is Feeling.

(2) Present a problem for them to solve. In presenting the problem, keep in mind the audience and their particular situation.

(3) Begin by setting up the following scenario:

Describe a lovely home that has just been built in a neighborhood, complete with a new garage. The owners have 2 adorable children. Describe how proud they are of their home.

Then describe a neighbor who has 2 boys and a large dog. The new home owners have a beautiful lawn, and the neighbor's dog Buster likes to bark a lot, and in addition, he likes to dig in the yard. The dog does not recognize property boundaries when he digs. The new owners think that the enjoyment of their home has been spoiled by the dog and the two boys. In addition they claim that the neighbor is never around to supervise the children and pet.

The neighbor is a single parent; she likes to send the boys next door in order to have some time alone. The neighbor explains that the boys really like going next door to play. It not only gives her some space, but exposes them to other adults, especially the dad. The dog, the neighbor says, is not tied up or confined so that he can roam the neighborhood and play with all the children.

When the new owners confront the neighbor, the neighbor goes on and on about how much fun the kids and the dog are having.

(4) Ask the Feeling types to share how they would solve the problem. Allow the group to process this information.

(5) Next, ask the Thinking types how they would solve this problem.

Developed by Sharon Lavoy.

(6) Ask the Thinking types to tell and process what is going on for them.

(7) Ask the Feeling types to do the same.

Hints about how the types may respond

Feeling types may want to build a fence or they may beat around the bush about the problem. They may be reticent about facing the issue head on.

Thinking types may be obviously seething. They almost always bring up leash laws. They also mention the potential liability for the homeowner of the children playing unsupervised in someone else's yard. They are irritated with the irresponsible attitude of the single parent.

Receiving a Gift

Purpose: To illustrate Thinking–Feeling differences in decision making.

Time: 15 to 20 minutes

Materials: Packages in 2 separate work areas (one for the Thinking group and one for the Feeling group). The packages should be beautifully wrapped with varying contents that can be shared (for example: licorice, box of cookies, suckers, package of paper clips, tea bags). Each area should have only enough packages for about 75 to 80 percent of the participants in that group.

Note pad, pen, envelope with instructions.

Process: (1) Divide the participants into two groups according to their preference for Thinking or Feeling. Tell each group that their instructions are in their separate work areas. Ask that one person record the dialogue of the group from beginning to end. Then send the two groups to their work areas.

(2) The instructions in the envelope should say something like this: "These gifts are for you. They are yours to keep. Sorry there aren't enough to go around. I know you will figure something out."

(3) Give the participants 10 minutes to work, then bring the groups together to share their dialogue and process. Discuss the differences between the groups.

Developed by Phyllis Threinen. (Reprinted with permission from *TYPEtype*, New Zealand.)

Published by the Center for Applications of Psychological Type

Hints about how the types may respond

Feeling types usually have a difficult time opening the packages for many reasons including that they don't want anyone to be left out and that they want everyone in harmony so they spend time trying to be fair. No one in the Feeling group wants to be perceived as the "bad guy" and often a few people will nobly step forward and opt to give up their share. Generally they will discuss giving everyone a chance to comment but may have a difficult time deciding who will open the gifts or how they will be divided. Often the Feeling types spend the allotted time figuring out how to be fair and never get the packages opened! Regardless of whether or not the packages get opened, the recorded dialogue helps illustrate the Feeling process. They often explain that they are feeling anxiety about the exercise; the dialogue may make it obvious that they can get stuck in the effort by trying to create harmony and to protect the feelings of others.

Thinking types usually cut to the chase. If the groups are in different rooms, the Ts often appear at the door munching on some of the treats from the packages while the Feelings types are still sorting out the process of being fair. The Thinking types often briefly talk about the various ways of splitting up the booty and quickly realize that nothing can be shared until they know what it is! Almost always the Ts will have everything ripped open and shared within the first three minutes after their logical analysis.

I tell executives that Thinking and Feeling
are like two TV channels or radio stations. You can
tune into logical content or what people care about.
If you only listen to one channel, you're missing
a lot of good information.

Catherine Fitzgerald

The Goodie Basket

Purpose: To demonstrate differences in the T–F process as influenced by Judging or Perceiving.

Time: Approximately 20 to 25 minutes.

Materials: A large basket (or box) with an assortment of inexpensive items (day calendars, rulers, kitchen aids, candy bars, key chains, deck of cards, pocket-sized books from grocery store, tiny screwdrivers to fix eyeglasses, etc.). There should be at least twice as many items as there are participants.

Paper, pens, and questions on a flip chart or overhead.

Process: (1) Tell the participants that there is a Goodie Basket. Everyone is to go to the basket and choose something from it. The item will be theirs. They are then to answer the following questions on a piece of paper:

- What did you choose?
- Why did you choose what you chose?
- Were you thinking of anyone else as you were choosing?
- Were you first, middle, or last to the basket?
- Did you have a difficult time choosing?

(2) Give everyone about 15 minutes to complete this portion of the exercise. Then have them put their answers away.

(3) Later, after they have received an explanation of type, have everyone take out their answer sheet and look at their answers with a knowledge of type. Discuss the answers and the processes. What they chose is not as important as why or how they made their decision in choosing.

Developed by Phyllis Threinen. (Reprinted with permission from *TYPEtype*, New Zealand.)

Published by the Center for Applications of Psychological Type

Hints about how the types may respond

Thinking types (especially TJs) are likely to be the first to the basket. They choose quickly, within seconds, with little difficulty. They do not give much thought to anyone else, either in the lineup or as a recipient of the gift. For them, it is a logical, direct decision. Once they have selected, they return to their place.

Feeling types tend to hang back, careful that others are able get their turn, sacrificing their options to choose first. FPs are the stragglers, the last to choose and the last to get back to the group. Many of the Fs also have someone in mind (a niece, daughter, brother, etc.) for whom they choose the gift.

Ps are generally the last ones left at the basket. In fact, you may find a P at the basket during a break, long after everyone else has chosen, considering a different item.

Often the Js will have picked something they can use relating to their dominant preference. They might choose a pocket-sized book on puzzles or quizzes or something related to organizing themselves. They are less likely to pick the "fun" stuff.

Ideal Relationship

Purpose: To demonstrate differences in what is valued by different types.

Time: 30 to 45 minutes

Materials: Flip-chart paper and markers.

Process: (1) Divide the larger group into four groups: ST, SF, NF, NT.

(2) Give the entire group the same assignment (write the following on a large sheet of newsprint):

Describe an ideal relationship.

(3) Send the four groups to different areas and have them come up with answers to the question as a group. Give them 10 to 15 minutes. Give them a sheet of newsprint and a marker to record their answers. (This exercise is most valuable if you can post the results, and compare and contrast the answers of the different groups.)

(4) Come back together as a large group and ask each group to hold up their newsprint and report on their group's results. For maximum contrast have them report out in the following order: ST, NF, SF, NT.

41

Planning a Workshop or Retreat

Purpose: To illustrate type differences in the planning process.

Time: 20 minutes

Materials: Flip-chart paper and markers.

Process: **(1)** Divide participants into small groups by ST, SF, NF, and NT. (If you have enough people, take other preferences and/or dominants into account.)

(2) Give each group a piece of flip-chart paper and magic markers. Tell them, "Your church group (club, class, etc.) is going to have a retreat (workshop, conference) this weekend. Start making plans. Write your plans on the piece of flip-chart paper." If a workshop/retreat/conference is not appropriate, have the groups plan a different event. Do not let yourself be drawn into any of the discussions. However, you should circulate, listening and watching both the process and the product.

Note: You should *not* give any further directions to assure that the differences between the groups will be sharper.

(3) After about 10 minutes, ask the groups to finish up and take their papers from them. Discuss the reports one group at a time, bringing out points that are typical of each type. Some of the things you should look for include the following:

- One group may number what they put on the paper, others won't.
- E groups may be louder.
- E or J groups may get to work more quickly or finish faster.
- S groups are likely to ask for more directions.
- Ns are not likely to ask for more directions.
- SF groups are more likely to think about the physical comfort of participants.
- NF groups are less likely to set a strict schedule; they will allow choices.
- One group, often Js and/or Ss will write down times; other groups won't.
- Ns are more likely to concern themselves with the theme of the retreat.
- I groups may do less writing.
- One group may be concerned with the colors of the markers that they use, and may even want to use more than one.
- One group, often Ns, may draw instead of write.

Developed by Barbara Reid and Jean Reid.

The Advertisement Exercise

This exercise can be used to test and strengthen understanding of the four function groups or temperaments because it focuses on key concerns and needs.

Purpose: To allow participants to test their understanding of the four function groups or temperaments.

Time: About an hour

Materials: A collection of printed advertisements that clearly appeal to the different function groups or temperaments. You may choose to use ads for the same thing, for instance, shoes, liquor, or vacations. Make this exercise as low-tech or high-tech as you desire.

Flip-chart paper and markers.

Example: Four shoe advertisements

- An ad that could be directed at NFs shows an outdoors shoe and says, "You promised Friday to the kids. We help you be ready for them."
- The NTs may prefer an ad picturing an elegant restaurant and a close-up of a shoe, with a line underneath, "When you've earned the right to the best, our legendary elegance will let everyone else know."
- An SF ad might play on loyalty to a company, "Stay with Nike. You know we won't let you down."
- The ST ad might be very practical, playing on the idea, "You can spend $200 on a pair of jogging shoes. But you can also get a pair of equal quality for only $69."

Process: (1) Divide the participants into function groups or temperament groups. The ideal group size includes 6–7 participants.

(2) Assign an advertisement to each group. Provide each group with flip-chart paper and markers.

Reprinted with permission from *TypeWorkS*.

Published by the Center for Applications of Psychological Type

(3) Ask each group to do the following (allow about 20 minutes):
   (a) Study the advertisement and decide whether it would appeal to the group members' preferences and why. If it does not appeal to the group's preferences, to which group might it appeal and why?

   (b) Alter the advertisement (or make up an entirely new one) to make it more appealing to the group's preferences. Encourage groups to get creative with the flip-chart paper and markers.

   (c) Prepare to present their findings to the other groups.

(4) Allow about 5 minutes for each group to report. Encourage other participants to comment or disagree with the group's conclusions. Correct any misunderstandings about type which become obvious during the discussion. Even when participants (and facilitators) cannot definitely agree about an ad, this exercise triggers some keen discussion about what appeals to whom.

(5) Summarize by pointing out that advertisers, even though they may not know about type, are obviously targeting different personalities in their advertisements.

Appreciation

Purpose: To demonstrate function pair differences and the diversity of reactions to recognition or acknowledgment.

Time: 30 to 45 minutes

Materials: Flip-chart paper and markers.

Process: (1) Divide participants into four groups: ST, SF, NF, NT.

(2) Assign the entire group to answer the following questions. Post the questions on a large sheet of flip-chart paper.
- *For what do you like to be appreciated?*
- *How do you like appreciation to be shown?*
- *If you don't receive appropriate appreciation, what happens to you?*

Sample answers are listed on the following page.

(3) Send the 4 groups to different areas and have each group discuss their answers to the questions. Give them 10 to 15 minutes. Give them a sheet of flip-chart paper and a marker to record their answers. This exercise is most valuable if you can post the results for all to see. It is important to discuss the differing needs and perspectives of each group.

(4) Come back together, and ask each group to report on their group's results. For maximum contrast, have them report in the following order: ST, NF, SF, NT.

Published by the Center for Applications of Psychological Type

Sample Answers to Appreciation Questions

NF

For what do you like to be appreciated?
- for a good job
- innovation
- effort and attitude
- originality
- how I relate to people
- knowledge

How do you like appreciation to be shown?
privately, not over done

NT

For what do you like to be appreciated?
- competence
- innovation
- new ideas
- overall accomplishment
- creative ways
- new solutions

How do you like appreciation to be shown?
simple, sincere, verbal content, taken
seriously with suggestions

SF

For what do you like to be appreciated?
- for the effort
- for a good job
- recognition that I'm doing it quietly
- for nonconventional manner
- that who I work with is more
important than what I do

How do you like appreciation to be shown?
one-on-one

ST

For what do you like to be appreciated?
- competence
- making good decisions
- accountability
- responsibility
- when I have done something that
inconveniences me

How do you like appreciation to be shown?
paycheck, shown materially, or verbally—
needs to be articulated so it matches what
was done, specific

Communication

Purpose: To identify communication patterns and learn to improve the communication process.

Time: 30 to 45 minutes

Materials: Flip-chart paper and markers. Suggested handout: *Talking in Type* (available from CAPT).

Process: (1) Divide participants into four groups: ST, SF, NF, NT.

(2) Assign the entire group to answer the following questions. Post the questions on a large sheet of flip-chart paper.

- *What is good communication?*
- *How do you like to be communicated with?*

(3) Send the four groups to different areas and ask each as a group to answer these questions within 10 to15 minutes. Give them a sheet of flip-chart paper and a marker to record their answers. This exercise is most valuable when you can post the results and compare and contrast the answers of the different groups.

(4) Reform the large group and ask each group to hold up its answers and report on the results. For maximum contrast, have the groups report in the following order: ST, NF, SF, NT.

(5) Sample responses:

ST: Paraphrasing, you repeat what I say and I repeat what you say to be sure we understand each other; we focus on the facts and don't let emotions get in the way; we agree to disagree; people are direct about the important content and don't beat around the bush; the communication is specific.

SF: We respect each other; we listen to each other's position; we work toward a harmonious outcome; we look for areas of agreement; we don't yell or hurt each other; we treat each other like people and take the time to connect.

NF: We work toward a common vision; we respect each other; we show concern for understanding the other person; we are honest, we look for

Published by the Center for Applications of Psychological Type

agreement and an inclusive solution, there is attention to what you say and also how you say it; even when there is disagreement there is still a caring context.

NT: The transfer of accurate content with as little noise as possible; there is high signal and low noise; there is a fair exchange of information; content, process, verbals, and nonverbals are taken into account; directness is important, "just tell me" without drama; we respect each other.

(6) As groups report, discuss similarities and differences. Typical patterns are noted below. Remember the patterns are all relative, though differences between ST, SF, NF, NT within the group as a whole are always apparent. The occupations and training of participants may influence results.

ST patterns: Behavioral descriptions of what constitutes good communication, focus on content/facts rather than "atmosphere" or relationship, more impersonal/direct.

SF patterns: Focus on listening, seeking of harmony, no hurt feelings, respecting/caring for each other from a "real people" perspective, very personal and relationship-oriented.

NF patterns: A more abstract sense of "getting along" with each other, ideals about how people "in general" should treat each other, a description of vague relationship qualities or atmosphere (vague to other types, not to NFs), concern for harmony and respect.

NT patterns: A more abstract, impersonal (often systemic) description with a few precise behaviors described, a "model" of good communication that incorporates "multiple levels" of communication (verbal, nonverbal, content, process, outcome), a matrix model in which ideas from all group members have been incorporated.

(7) Point out to the group that there are some fundamental differences in the ways they define communication. You might say something such as "If we don't define it in the same way, is it any surprise that we have trouble making it happen?" Ask the group how they can integrate elements from these different definitions to improve communication in their group.

Variations: **(A)** How do you bring about good communication (on a team, at work, etc)?

(B) What are barriers to communication?

(C) What is good feedback?

Investigating Conflict

This exercise can be used in many ways to investigate attitudes and approaches to conflict. Typically only some of the questions are used, depending on the facilitator's objectives, training design, and time constraints.

Purpose: To compare similarities and differences in definitions and reactions to conflict. To learn strategies, based on an understanding of type differences, to use in resolving conflicts.

Time: 30 minutes

Materials: Flip-chart paper and markers.

Process: (1) Divide participants into paired function groups (ST, SF, NT, NF). Give each group sheets of flip-chart paper and a marker and ask the groups to record their responses to the following:

Define conflict.

(2) How do members of your group typically react to conflict? (How do they behave in a conflict situation?)

(3) How should others approach members of your group if they want to solve a conflict with them?

(4) Describe the common sources of conflict for people in your group. (You may want to describe to one another recent conflicts you have had and what you believe the source of the conflict was.)

(5) Which types of conflict are most upsetting to the members of your group?

(6) What approaches do members of your group typically use to try to solve conflicts?

Adapted from *Psychological Type in Schools: Applications for Educators* by Sondra VanSant and Diane Payne. Used with permission.

Published by the Center for Applications of Psychological Type

Notes: All groups should respond to at least questions 1, 2, and 3. You may wish to give each group additional questions as time allows. After the time allotted for the activity, ask each group to share its report with the entire group.

In the debriefing, you may wish to ask questions such as the following:

(1) What similarities and differences did you notice among the groups' definitions of conflict?

(2) Compare and contrast sources of conflict and reactions to conflict based on type differences.

(3) What did you experience as you did this exercise?

(4) How would you characterize the key features of each group regarding conflict, based on your experience in this exercise?

(5) How can you apply what you learned in the exercise to effectively handle conflict situations?

Variations: (A) Ask STs and NFs to discuss appropriate ways they might handle conflict between their types.

(B) Ask SFs and NTs to discuss appropriate ways they might handle conflict between their types.

Management

Purpose: To discover how different types prefer to be managed.

Time: 30 to 45 minutes

Materials: Flip-chart paper and markers. Suggested handout: *Management Implications of Type* (available from CAPT).

Process: (1) Divide participants into four groups: ST, SF, NF, NT.

(2) Assign the entire group to answer the following question. Post the question on a large sheet of flip-chart paper.

How do you like to be managed (supervised)?

(3) Send the 4 groups to different areas and have them come up, as a group, with answers to this question. Give them 10 to 15 minutes. Give them a sheet of flip-chart paper and a marker to record their answers. This exercise is most valuable if you can post the results and compare/contrast the answers of the different groups.

(4) Come back together as a large group and ask each group to hold up its answers and report on the results. For maximum contrast have them report in the following order: ST, NF, SF, NT.

Published by the Center for Applications of Psychological Type

Type and Work

This exercise offers an opportunity for type trainers to demonstrate differences in how individuals perceive and experience work. It was developed as a result of observations by workshop participants about their experiences in the workplace, as well as in the career decision-making phase.

Purpose: To provide an opportunity for workshop participants to experience type differences in how individuals with varying mental process combinations experience a variety of work issues.

To develop an understanding of key issues regarding forces working for creating compatibility and self-esteem among different individuals.

For groups with advanced understanding of the MBTI instrument this exercise can be used to demonstrate type dynamics, as well as the differences between individuals of different dominant functions.

Time: 30 to 45 minutes

Materials: Flip-chart paper and markers. Suggested handout: *Contributions Made by Each Preference to Each Type* (available from CAPT).

Process: (1) Explain to participants that different combinations of the mental processes offer an excellent and practical opportunity to view differences in how the workplace is experienced. Tell them that the following exercise is designed to help them see these differences as well as gain insight into how they might help individuals meet their needs in the workplace.

(2) Group participants based on their preferred attitude combinations ST, SF, NF, NT. If you have adequate numbers, groups can be structured around dominant and auxiliary combinations.

(3) Give participants the worksheet titled *MBTI Work Exercise* on the following page, a piece of flip-chart paper, and a marker. Allow them 20 minutes to work through the worksheet, asking them to identify a recorder to report back to the larger group later.

(4) Allow about 4 to 5 minutes for each group to share its observations.

(5) Summarize the contrasts provided by individual groups.

Developed by Scott Anchors.

MBTI Work Exercise

(1) For my type, work is a reflection of:

(2) For my type, the most important contribution I can make in my work situation is:

(3) In our work we like to be rewarded for:

(4) The worst thing I can be asked to do in a job is:

Published by the Center for Applications of Psychological Type

The Merit or Worth

Purpose: To demonstrate the criteria different function groups use for assessing the value of something.

Time: 30 minutes

Materials: Flip-chart paper and markers.

Process: **(1)** Divide participants into function groups (ST, SF, NT, NF). If any group is too large, divide it into smaller groups.

(2) Ask each group how it decides whether something is valuable or has merit. Have each group write its answers on the flip-chart paper.

(3) Have each group present its report to the entire group and discuss the differences and similarities.

A J–P Fishbowl

Purpose: To point out differences between the Judging and Perceiving preferences.

Time: About 20 to 25 minutes

Materials: None, or list of things to watch for (see process).

Process: (1) Ask all Js (5 or 6 if the total group is large) to bring their chairs to the center or front of the room while the others sit around the outside of the circle.

(2) Then ask those *inside* the fishbowl a question, such as "Are relationships in our society changing? If so, how? If not, why not?" (A question can be picked to suit the group and should be something that the group cares about.) Let the small group in the fishbowl discuss the question.

Before the Js start the discussion, ask the people *outside* the fishbowl to watch for the following as the discussion proceeds:
- kinds of interaction
- dynamics
- body language
- words used and definitions of those words
- use of words and gestures

(3) Allow about 5 minutes for the discussion.

(4) Repeat steps 1 to 3, but this time have a group of Ps discuss the question.

(5) Then ask the whole group what differences they noticed between the groups. Point out anything that the observers miss.

Hints about how the two groups respond

The Js will usually make an immediate judgment and then go on to support it. Their words will be definite and clear-cut. They will tend to lean towards each other. They may use arm gestures to emphasize point.

Ps will address all sides of the question. They may have a more difficult time getting the discussion started. They will most likely not come to a decision. Their body language tends to be more relaxed and they may lean back in their chairs.

Developed by Eve Delunas.

Work, Play, and Type

This exercise reveals attitudes and areas of conflict surrounding work and play, related to MBTI preferences. The clearest differences in work and play attitudes are reflected on the J–P scale. This exercise can be used after explaining the four preferences to further clarify J–P differences. Other uses of the exercise are in human resources development, marriage and family counseling, and personal growth workshops.

Purpose: To recognize differences in how the Judging and Perceiving types view work and play.

Time: 15 minutes

Materials: None.

Process: (1) Tell everyone to picture an imaginary line running horizontally along one wall or diagonally across the room from one corner to another.

(2) This imaginary line is a work-play continuum. On one end is the position: "Work should be finished before playing" (or "I can't play if my work isn't done"). On the other end is the position: "Playing is OK anytime" (or "I can play regardless of my work").

(3) Ask participants to think about where they would put themselves on this imaginary line/continuum. Each person should get up and stand at the point on the line that reflects his or her position.

(4) After milling has ceased and people have established their positions standing along the line, use some or all of these questions to process the exercise:

- What are the types at the two ends of the line? Are there any patterns in type distribution along the line?
- Would some people be willing to share why they chose that particular point on the line?
- How do people feel about the place where they are standing? Do they like it? Would they like to move?
- Ask the two ends of the line to debate with each other about the merits of their positions with you as referee. (Usually this becomes a J vs. P dialogue.)
- What have you learned about yourself, others, and type?

Star and Sailboat

Purpose: To demonstrate the differences between the Judging and Perceiving preferences.

Time: 10 to 15 minutes

Materials: Box of arts and crafts supplies (paper, glue, markers, fabric, tape measures, rope, wood scraps, scissors, yarn, straws, and any other art supplies.)

Process: (1) Divide into J and P groups with 5 or 6 members in each group. Place the box of supplies in the center of the room.

(2) Tell the groups that they have 5 minutes to make the best star they can make. They can use any materials they want from the box or they can choose to use nothing from the box. They can use anything they have with them; there are no restrictions. Tell them that at the end of 5 minutes you will judge which star is the best and that group will be the winner.

(3) At the end of 3 1/2 minutes, announce that you have changed your mind and that you want them to make a sailboat instead. Tell them that they have one minute left. You can imagine the reaction!

(4) After the minute, debrief the participants.

Hints about how the types may respond

The Js usually spend a great deal of the last minute either complaining or panicking. They will often want to show the excellent star that they had almost finished—sometimes with angles precisely measured.

The Ps, on the other hand, usually finish the sailboat and find the whole exercise to be quite fun. Some Ps may choose to use no materials at all to create either object, but instead create a human sculpture.

Developed by Candice Johnson.

Different Is Good:
An Exploration of Types in the Workplace

Purpose: To have participants shift their focus from clarifying their own types to working with people of other preferences.

Time: About 60 minutes

Materials: Copies or overheads of the situations.

Process: **(1)** Divide the class into four groups, one for each pair of preferences (E–I, S–N, T–F, J–P). To the degree possible, pick people who have very clear preferences in the pair their group will work with. This helps the differences show up clearly during the exercise. Assign the following situations appropriately to each group.

(2) Have participants work 5- to 10-minutes *individually* to respond in writing to the situation assigned to them. Ask them also to read the other three situations.

(3) Have groups work for 15- to 20-minutes *together* to **(a)** compare responses of the members, and **(b)** to generate ideas for how to work effectively with each preference in the pair assigned to each group.

(4) Have the groups report for about 30 minutes total. If a group has lots of ideas for one preference in the pair, try to bring out some ideas for the other preference so that people have tips for dealing with each preference. For example, if the S–N group brings out many interesting ideas for working with Sensing types and few ideas for Intuitive types, then guide the discussion to bring out ideas for working with Intuitives. Important learning can come from describing the process the group used as well as from the conclusions reached.

(5) Summarize by saying that participants now have ways to see how type knowledge can be applied in everyday situations.

Situations:
(1) Extravert–Introvert: You scored as an Introvert and you have to work with an Extravert on a project. What are some important points you want to keep in mind as you communicate with the Extravert?

(2) Sensing–Intuition: You have a preference for Intuition but now find yourself on a team with a strong Sensing type who is very satisfied with the way the

Reprinted with permission from *TypeWorkS*. Adapted from TeamPac, copyright 1994, IBM, Corp.

team is currently working. You think some changes need to occur. What can you do to enlist the Sensing type's support for your plans?

(3) Thinking–Feeling: You have preferences for Thinking and a fellow team member has just told you that another team member, who scores as a Feeling type, does not trust you. What can you do to try to establish trust with the Feeling decision maker?

(4) Judging–Perceiving: You have a preference for Perceiving. Just as your team has made a decision about the problem you have been discussing in a team meeting, you think of another entirely different way to approach and solve the problem. What can you do about your idea to keep the Judging types on your team from becoming irritated that you are not yet ready to go with the team's decision?

That Says It All

This fun exercise is an excellent way to summarize discussion of one preference or of all 4 preference pairs. Use it also to examine important qualities for each of the 16 types.

Purpose: To test and deepen understanding of type by having participants capture the essence of a preference or type in a motto or saying.

Time: 20 to 30 minutes

Materials: Flip-chart paper and markers.

Process: (1) Divide the class into groups of 4 or 5 people. If teaching one preference pair, make several groups for each preference. If examining all preferences, then use one group for each pair of preferences (E–I, S–N, T–F, J–P) and ask each group to generate two mottos, one for each preference.

(2) Explain the exercise by providing examples. A traditional motto for Feeling types might be, "A spoonful of sugar makes the medicine go down." A new motto for Judging types could be, "Never put off to tomorrow a decision that can be made today."

(3) Ask each group to create at least one motto for the preference(s) assigned. The mottos can be existing ones, but groups seem to prefer new versions. Allow 10 to 15 minutes, but monitor progress and end the work time when appropriate.

(4) Ask each small group to share its motto(s) and ask for reactions. Some mottos generate discussion or need clarification (an excellent way to uncover lingering misunderstanding). Others simply bring laughter and appreciation.

(5) Have each group post its results on the wall. Leave these up and let participants know they can add additional mottos during the workshop.

Variation: This exercise can also be done individually, usually to examine individual types. Although this solo work creates less energy, it is a good way to have individuals think through the essence of their types. In very large classes, you may have enough types to create whole type groups and proceed as a group exercise.

Reprinted with permission from *TypeWorkS*.

The Want Ad Exercise

Purpose: To introduce the concept of job and type match and to increase understanding of a given preference pair or of whole types.

Time: 60 to 90 minutes

Materials: Want ads collected from newspapers, magazines, jobs posted, etc.

Process: (1) Review the following two options before the workshop and decide which one you will use. Collect want ads. These should be appropriate to the participants' interests and fairly detailed. If print is very small, enlarge the ads or copy as handouts. For easy handling, want ads can be presented on index cards.

(2) In the workshop, introduce the purpose and process of the exercise.

(3) **For one large group:** Display or hand out a want ad. Lead a discussion by asking the group the following questions:

 (a) *What type (or preference) would find this job appealing? Why?*

 (b) *Why would other types (or preferences) find this job unappealing or difficult? What changes or approaches could be used to make the job a better fit for them?*

For beginners or predominantly Sensing groups, you may need to provide examples of how to alter jobs (question b). During this discussion, correct misunderstandings as they arise and model the process you want people to use.

It is important to note that people should not select jobs solely based on type, and that employers should never use type as a basis for hiring.

Discussion of each want ad should take about 20 minutes. Use at least three ads to be sure everyone understands the principles of fit between type and job.

(4) **For small groups:** Explain the task (using the same two questions for the large group) to the groups and assign a want ad(s) to each. (If you want to focus on a certain preference, tell each group). Allow 20 minutes for group discussion.

Circulate as the groups work to be sure they understand the assignment and stay on track. Ask groups to share their conclusions. Process questions, commenting as necessary to clarify points.

Reprinted with permission from *TypeWorkS*.

Published by the Center for Applications of Psychological Type

Group Tasks and Type

Purpose: To have participants use their knowledge of type preferences and apply it to understanding some of their group's potential strengths and weaknesses.

Time: 30 minutes to one hour depending on the size of the group

Materials: Copies of worksheets on the following pages.

Process: (1) Explain to participants that although individuals have a preference for one side of each of these pairs, most also use their nonpreferred sides to accomplish daily tasks. In like manner, the tasks of a group may call on one preference or another, but all preferences are used to accomplish the work.

(2) Say that the exercise asks participants to identify tasks that require group members to exercise skills associated with each preference. By analyzing these tasks and the type preferences of the group members, participants will be able to identify group strengths, weaknesses, and ways to enhance the effectiveness of the group.

(3) Tell participants to follow the instructions on the worksheets to complete their analyses.

> Even though we each have a preferred way of being on four of the MBTI scales, it is important to remember that we could not function if we did not frequently use all of the functions and attitudes.

Developed by Adam Yagodka and Susan Clancy.

Task List

In order to complete the attached exercise, you will need to list the tasks your work group or organization performs. If possible, state each task starting with an action verb, i.e., "Sets policy for . . . ," "Gathers budget data for . . . ," etc.

List at least 10 tasks. When you have completed this task list, follow the instructions on the next page.

_____

_____

_____

_____

_____

_____

_____

_____

_____

_____

_____

_____

_____

_____

_____

_____

_____

_____

Published by the Center for Applications of Psychological Type

Task Relationships with Type Constructs

Identify and list the work group or organizational tasks that might require skills associated with each of the following preferences. Then answer the questions on the following page.

EXTRAVERSION

INTROVERSION

SENSING

INTUITION

THINKING

FEELING

JUDGMENT

PERCEPTION

Questions

(1) Go back and underline those tasks you feel the group does very well.

(2) Circle those tasks you feel the group does not do well.

(3) Look at the underlined tasks. Into which type boxes do they fall? How does this information compare to the group's type profile?

(4) Look at the tasks that are circled. Into which type boxes do they fall? How does this information compare to the group's type profile?

(5) List any important tasks that are missing. Into which boxes would they belong? Are these tasks associated with aspects of type not well represented by the group, i.e., boxes in which few members show a preference?

(6) Compare the type preference of the group's leader(s) to the group's strengths (underlined tasks) and weaknesses (circled tasks). How do they compare?

(7) Using your knowledge of type, how would you consider reinforcing the group's strengths and deal with the group's weaknesses?

(8) How can you best use your type to enhance the effectiveness of the group?

Published by the Center for Applications of Psychological Type

Change

Purpose: To demonstrate the differences between types in their attitudes toward change.

Time: 30 minutes or more, depending on the discussion of the answers.

Materials: Flip-chart paper and overhead or handout with questions.

Process: (1) Divide the participants into groups by IS, IN, ES, and EN preferences. Ask the groups to discuss the following questions and write down their answers.

- How do you feel about change?
- How can someone convince you to change or that change is needed?
- How can someone convince you that change is not needed?

(2) Ask each group to present its answers. Begin with either the IS group or the EN group, as these two provide the most contrast. Then let the IN group and the ES group present. Discuss the similarities and differences.

Hints about how the types may respond

The ISs are likely to say that they do not like change. Remind the group that the ISs are the people who are most interested in the traditions of an organization and will protect those traditions. (If it's worked before, it should work again.)

The ENs are likely to say that they *love* change. They are constantly looking for change and variety, for new ways of doing things. They are oriented toward the outside world.

The ESs share some of the qualities of each of the other groups. They are much less likely to want change than the ENs, but are more willing to change than the ISs.

The INs have a strong sense of the tradition of an organization but are much more willing to change than the ISs.

Conflict Resolution

Purpose: To demonstrate type differences and how they affect reactions to conflict.

Time: 30 to 35 minutes

Materials: Flip-chart paper and markers.

Process: (1) Divide participants into IF, IT, EF, ET groups and ask them to respond to the following questions and statements:

- Define conflict.
- How do you deal with conflict?
  - Internally?
  - Externally?
- How do you want to be approached in a conflict situation?
- What does resolution mean to you?

(2) Ask participants to post their answers on flip-chart paper and to have a spokesperson. Allow about 15 to 20 minutes for them to answer the questions. Allow time for discussion. Contrast and compare answers.

(3) You may want to show the conflict-resolution model on the following page. Discuss where each group believes its type belongs.

Published by the Center for Applications of Psychological Type

Model For Conflict Resolution*

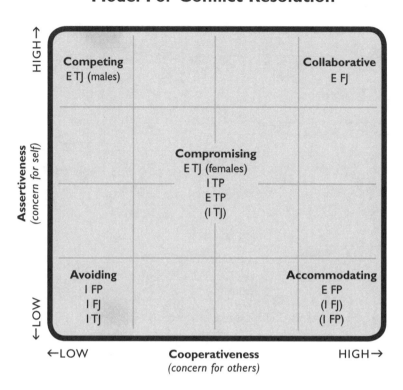

Most Preferred Conflict-Handling Strategy

Thinking Dominant

E TJ   Compete
(Males)

E TJ   Compromise
(Females)

I TP   Compromise

Thinking Auxiliary

E TP   Compromise

I TJ   Avoid (and if not able to do so, then compromise)

Feeling Dominant

E FJ   Collaborate

I FP   Avoid (and if not able to do so, then accommodate)

Feeling Auxiliary

E FP   Accommodate

I FJ   Avoid (and if not able to do so, then accommodate)

*Based on: Percival, T. Q., Smitheram, V., & Kelly, M. (1992). Myers-Briggs Type Indicator and conflict-handling intention: An interactive approach. *Journal of Psychological Type, 23,* 10–16.

Vacation Planning

Purpose: To increase your knowledge of preferences and learn to value the strengths of other preferences.

Time: 20 to 30 minutes

Materials: Flip-chart paper and markers.

Process: (1) Divide participants into 4 groups: EJ, EP, IJ, IP.

(2) Ask each group to discuss how its members plan a vacation and to record the answers on the flip-chart paper.

(3) Ask each group to report and discuss the differences and similarities.

Published by the Center for Applications of Psychological Type

Decision-Making Process

Purpose: To demonstrate how people with varying preference combinations experience decision making and to solicit ideas and suggestions to assist individuals through the decision-making process.

Time: 60 minutes

Materials: Flip-chart paper and markers.

Process: (1) Introduce the exercise by saying, "Different combinations of the attitudes offer an excellent and practical opportunity to view the rich decision-making approach and process of different types. The following exercise is designed to help you see these differences as well as gain insight into strategies that might be useful in working with individuals in the decision-making arena."

(2) Place group participants into attitude combinations (EJ, EP, IJ, IP).

(3) Ask these groups to discuss the following questions and be prepared to report back to the larger group. Give groups about 20 minutes to work.

- What process do you go through in making a decision?
- What is this like for you?
- What forces work for and against you in this process?
- What strategies or suggestions might help people with this attitude pair reach closure on a decision?

(4) Debrief each group and make appropriate notes on a flip chart. Allow 4 to 5 minutes per group. Asking the groups to report in the order of EJ, EP, IJ, and IP usually provides the optimal contrast between groups on the issue of decision making.

Encourage participants to ask questions and comment on the reports. If a group makes a point that normally does not come from that attitude pair, probe for more information on that point and the connection with attitudes. Group members may also explain why their group came up with any given point.

(5) At the end of each report, summarize briefly and point out the contrasts with groups who have already reported.

Developed by Scott Anchors.

Teaching Exercise

Purpose: Learning how to communicate with people with other preferences.

Time: 30 to 45 minutes

Materials: Groups may request flip-chart paper, erase boards, or other materials to use in their lessons.

Process: (1) Divide the group into dominant-alike groups.

Teachers: Have each group design a lesson plan to teach something to the rest of the class. (For example, how to add fractions with like denominators.)

Others: Have groups plan how they would teach something to a new employee in their company.

(2) Have each group actually teach its lesson.

(3) Debrief the exercise by having the other participants indicate to each group of presenters what they found particularly helpful about the presentation. Also ask them to share what they missed—what would have made the presentation clearer or more interesting.

Lots of good ideas invariably surface during the debriefing time and participants are exposed to lots of different strategies and methodologies during the presentations.

Developed by Candice Johnson.

Published by the Center for Applications of Psychological Type

Guided Fantasy Trip

Purpose: To demonstrate the differences and richness of how types take in and respond to information.

Time: 20 to 30 minutes

Materials: Flip-chart paper and markers.

Process: (1) Ask participants to relax and close their eyes. Tell the group the story of an imaginary trip. Present opportunities for discovering objects, house environments, people, places, etc.

(2) End the trip. Divide into type-alike or function groups and have them discuss what they "saw" and record on flip-chart paper.

(3) Have each group report back to the whole group. As each group reports, point out similarities and differences in what was discussed and recorded.

Developed by Eve Delunas.

Important People

Purpose: To demonstrate type differences.

Time: 10 to 15 minutes

Materials: Flip-chart paper and markers.

Process: (1) Divide participants into type-alike groups. Ask each group to decide on three persons who are very important to the world and tell why. Have groups list the people on the flip-chart paper.

(2) Have each group report back to the whole group. As each group reports, point out similarities and differences in what was discussed and recorded as it relates to type.

Developed by Eve Delunas.

Published by the Center for Applications of Psychological Type

Likes/Dislikes

Purpose: To point out type preference differences.

Time: 30 minutes

Materials: Flip-chart paper and markers.

Process: *For Group Activity:*

(1) Divide participants into groups. Depending on the number of participants, divide into type-alike, cousin type, or function groups.

(2) Give the group the following questions and statements to answer or complete:

"Something that I do that drives others crazy is _____."

"Something that others do that I dislike very much is _____."

"What do you imagine would be the best possible way of life? Worst?"

Ask groups to record their answers on flip-chart paper.

(3) Have each group report to the whole group. As each group reports, point out similarities and differences in what was discussed and recorded.

For Individual Activity:

(1) Give each person some blank paper.

(2) Ask individuals to respond to the following questions either by drawing or writing. Use a separate sheet of paper for each.

"Something that I do that really drives others crazy is _____."

"Something that others do that I really dislike very much is _____."

"What do you imagine would be the best possible way of life? Worst?"

(3) Have individuals report to the whole group. As each person reports, point out similarities and differences in what was not discussed, only recorded.

Developed by Eve Delunas.

A Class Starter

A good exercise for building cohesion.

Purpose: Clarifying understanding of own type and others.

Time: Depends on the number of different types that are represented.

Materials: Type descriptions from computer-generated type reports, type descriptions from *Descriptions of the Sixteen Types* or *Looking At Type®: The Fundamentals* or other sources.

Process: (1) Divide participants into type-alike groups. Have each group decide on two things that the group wants the world to know about its type and record them on paper.

(2) Have each group report back to the whole group. As each group reports, point out similarities and differences in what was discussed and recorded.

Developed by Eve Delunas.

Published by the Center for Applications of Psychological Type

Difficult Students

Purpose: Increase awareness of possible bias and type blindness; understand the role type differences play in the student-educator professional relationship; and use type knowledge to formulate strategies for reducing these difficulties in the helping process.

Time: 30 to 45 minutes

Materials: Flip-chart paper and markers.

Process: (1) Say the following to the group: "Think about the kinds of students you have found most difficult or frustrating to work with (or students whose progress has been unsatisfying for you). Make some notes for yourself right now about the characteristics of these difficult students. Note any MBTI patterns you discern. It may help to think of several specific individuals you have worked with recently." (Allow 5 to 10 minutes.)

(2) Divide participants into type-alike groups, and ask them to appoint a reporter to write down patterns within the group as each person shares from his or her notes. Have participants discuss how their comments relate to type and in what ways. (Allow 10 to 15 minutes.)

(3) Call the group back together, and process the activity by calling on each reporter. If distinct type patterns emerge, create a dialogue between the types having difficulty with each other. For example: the ENFP group may list frustrations with SJs. The SJs can then be asked to react to the ENFP report with suggestions for bridging difficulties, or the SJs and ENFPs can be grouped for a discussion, as can other groups.

Summary: Observe patterns, make points about professionals being limited by their own types, and explain the importance of understanding expectations, needs, and differences of the 16 types as students.

Verifying Types in Type-Alike Groups

Purpose: To verify type.

Time: 45 to 90 minutes (depending on how many different types are represented in the group of participants).

Materials: Participants' report forms, markers, flip-chart paper.

Process: (1) Tell the participants that the purpose of this exercise is for them to discuss their MBTI reports with others who came out the same type. This helps them discover how valid type theory and the results of the MBTI instrument are for them.

(2) Divide into type-alike groups.

(3) Ask participants to read their reports and discuss them in any way the group wishes. Tell them to look for agreement and disagreement. Suggest that they go beyond the MBTI results. Do they see other similarities? Do members feel as if they fit in the group they are in?

Sometimes the group discussion helps people realize that their MBTI reports don't fit and that they may belong with different groups.

(4) Give each group a piece of paper and a marker. Tell the groups to put their four letters at the top of the page. Then write their agreements and discoveries on the paper.

(5) Have a member of each group read the report with any other comments the group suggests.

(6) Put the reports on the wall with masking tape so they can be referred to during the rest of the workshop.

Published by the Center for Applications of Psychological Type

Which Is Our Song?

This exercise appeals to Sensing types as well as Intuitive types. It is a nice change of pace and Perceiving types like the spontaneity. People may claim they "can't carry a tune," but they soon get caught up in the spirit of the activity.

Purpose: To allow participants to capture the essence of preferences or temperaments.

Time: 30 to 40 minutes, depending on the number of groups.

Materials: Flip-chart paper or overheads for each group with markers.

Process: (1) Divide the class into groups of 4 or 5, assigning a preference or temperament to each group, depending on how you are using the exercise. Ideally people are grouped by their real preferences or temperaments. Some adjustment can be made if groups are very uneven.

(2) Ask each group to pick or create a song to illustrate its assigned preference or temperament. The song might even illustrate the differences between two preferences. Groups can use existing songs or existing tunes with new lyrics. Each group should be prepared to sing its song for the rest of the class.

(3) Provide the groups with a few examples so they understand what is expected. You can mention "My Favorite Things" as an S song or "Some Enchanted Evening" for Ns. Most groups will probably choose existing tunes and invent new lyrics. Some groups use nursery rhymes. You can even ask a few lively participants to sing a line or two of an invented song from an earlier session to give people the idea. Here is an example you can use:
  (To the tune of *O Tannenbaum*)
  "O Extraverts, O Extraverts, you laugh aloud, you're so alert.
  You talk it out, you think aloud; you're mostly happy in a crowd."

(4) Allow 10 to 15 minutes for groups to work. Ask groups to write their lyrics on flip-chart paper or overheads.

(5) Have each group perform its song. Some groups may want to just read the words, but if you gently insist they perform, much more energy and fun is created. Or the whole class can sing from the displayed lyrics.

(6) Encourage discussion, comments, or suggestions about each song's message and how it links to the assigned preference or temperament. If the exercise points out any misunderstanding about the preferences or temperaments, be sure to address it.

Reprinted with permission from *TypeWorkS.*

Problem Solving

Purpose: Appreciate how each of the four functions works in the problem-solving process; identify most and least preferred functions and then see the implications of these preferences in the problem-solving process; compare process with that of someone with an opposite type.

Time: 30 minutes

Materials: Graph paper, copies of *Looking at Type®: The Fundamentals*.

Process: (1) Read together pages 55 and 56 of *Looking at Type®: The Fundamentals*, "Problem Solving."

(2) Ask each person to list their dominant, auxiliary, tertiary, and inferior (#1, #2, #3, #4) functions. Now put the following number of points next to each function: #1 Dominant = 14 points, #2 Auxiliary = 9 points, #3 Tertiary = 5 points, #4 Inferior = 2 points.

(3) Using a strip of graph paper, have each participant start with S and color in the number of blocks that corresponds to the points listed in the previous step. Then in the following sequence, do the same for N, T, and F.

(4) Circulate to make sure everyone understands the procedure.

(5) Now have people take their strips of graph paper and line them up with those of people of opposite types (in pairs or trios) and spend 10 minutes discussing the implications of their decision-making processes. What would it be like to work with this person or live together and make decisions? What would be the strengths and conflicts?

(6) Process the whole group and elicit application ideas for this exercise and its implications.

Developed by Judith Provost.

Draw Your Lifeline

Purpose: To demonstrate a technique for evaluating one's life in terms of highs and lows and in terms of circumstances that encouraged and discouraged type development.

Time: 45 minutes to one hour

Materials: Paper and pencil for each person.

Process: (1) Give participants an 8 1/2 × 11 sheet of paper and ask them to draw a line to divide it in half horizontally. Tell them to mark the line with the following stages:

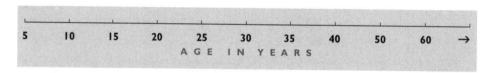

(2) Next, ask them to jot down for each age what immediately comes to mind for these questions:

- Above the line: What was significant for you in a positive way?
- Below the line: What was significant for you in a negative way?

Allow about 10 minutes.

(3) Then ask them to mark their MBTI preferences next to events/things related to that preference. Explain that these could have stimulated, satisfied, or discouraged their type. Allow about five minutes.

(4) Instruct the participants to find someone they don't know, of like type, and share as much as they are comfortable sharing from their lifeline. Allow 10 minutes for each person.

(5) Process exercise with the whole group:

- How did you respond to this activity?
- Did you notice any patterns in your lifeline related to type?
- How does your lifeline fit, or not fit, with type development theory?

Developed by Judith Provost.

EXERCISE

Firing/Raises

Purpose: To demonstrate type differences in a work situation.

Time: 10 to 15 minutes

Materials: None.

Process: (1) This is a fishbowl exercise. Ask for two volunteers of different types.

(2) Have each of the people role-play the act of firing someone.

(3) Have the whole group discuss and point out similarities and differences, and strengths and weakness in what they observed.

Variation: For step 2, substitute having each person ask for a raise. Some types have a very hard time asking for a raise and saying why they deserve it. NFs often have the worst time.

A frequent mistake intuitive types make in communicating about change is to assume that the amount of information that convinced them of the need for change will be sufficient for the sensing type.

Sue G. Clancy, Developing Leaders

Developed by Eve Delunas.

Published by the Center for Applications of Psychological Type

Communication Strategies Worksheet

Purpose: To use type knowledge to improve communications skills.

Time: 15 to 20 minutes

Materials: Suggested handout: *The Four-Part Framework* (available from CAPT).

Process: **(1)** Ask each participant to complete the following information:
I believe that my type preference is: _____ (or best guess for now).
The name of the person that I'd like to build my communication with
is: _____ .

Using *The Four-Part Framework,* by observing the person's behavior I would
guess that their type preferences are:

E (talk it out)   I (think it through)
S (specifics)   N (big picture)
T (logical implications)   F (impact on people)
J (joy of closure)   P (joy of processing)

What strengths do you see this person using?

What gets in your way when trying to communicate effectively with this
person? Does it appear related to type preferences?

What strategies does the type framework suggest that you might use to
communicate more effectively?

(2) Ask for volunteers to share their answers and use these examples to help
participants process and apply this information to their own circumstances.

Developed by Susan Brock.

Cutting Up

The physical activity involved in making a collage to illustrate types or preferences makes this exercise a good change of pace for workshops. This hands-on activity can be used to show individual preferences, whole types, temperaments, even function pairs or dominants. It can be used effectively with work teams or as a wrap-up activity for workshops.

Purpose: To allow participants to visually show type differences.

Time: 40 to 50 minutes

Materials: A large piece of posterboard, flip-chart paper, cardboard, or foamboard as a base for each collage. You will need a wide variety of materials for making the collages: magazines or catalogs as sources for cutting out words or pictures, other creative materials such as string, ribbons, wallpapers, stickers, markers, crayons, and several pairs of scissors, as well as glue and tape.

Process: (1) Divide participants into type, temperament, or preference groups. This exercise can also be done by individuals. Ask groups or individuals to create with the available materials a collage of materials, images, or words that illustrates or symbolizes their preferences.

(2) Have groups or individuals present the collage to the whole group and discuss how it reflects their preference. Encourage questions and comments from others.

Variations: (A) When complete, collages can be posted with only the type of the artist(s) noted. Allow time for viewing by all participants. Then ask participants to share their reactions.

(B) If you feel adventuresome, try tailoring this activity to reflect special subject matter. For example, if you are focusing on the inferior function, try asking that the collage reflect the inferior function for the assigned type. The same might be done with such topics as attitude to conflict, role in teams, or type of leadership preferred. If you do try a new version, be prepared to be flexible and shift the focus if you see groups are having problems.

Reprinted with permission from *TypeWorkS*.

Published by the Center for Applications of Psychological Type

Career Choices

Purpose: To help participants understand type differences in the area of career search.

Time: 10 to 15 minutes

Materials: None.

Process: (1) Place participants in dyads with different types. Tell participants that they are going to be in a job interview.

(2) Give each person time to play both the employer and the prospective employee. Prospective employees should be sure to tell what their strengths and weaknesses are (in light of type profile), and how the employer can capitalize on their strengths and help them to avoid using (or to develop) their weaker areas (less well-developed preferences).

(3) Ask the people role-playing prospective employees to talk about people they work well with (e.g., a P may like to work with a J, who will encourage the P to closure, or an N may enjoy working with an S, who is on top of the details).

Developed by Eve Delunas.

An Introductory Dyad

This introductory dyad, according to the presenter, is better than alcohol for getting people acquainted!

Purpose: To think about and appreciate different types.

Time: 15 to 20 minutes depending on the size of the group.

Materials: Individual type descriptions scoring profiles for each participant.

Process: (1) After an explanation of the preferences, give type descriptions to each of the participants and have them read and study their own profiles individually.

(2) Then have each one pair off with any other type and do one of the following:
   (a) Find two things in the profiles that are alike and two things that are unlike.
   (b) Find two things from the profile that they believe others don't usually know about their type.

Developed by Eve Delunas.

Published by the Center for Applications of Psychological Type

Lifeboat

This exercise is recommended for groups in which the members are comfortable with each other. Facilitators are cautioned to help participants work through feelings during the exercise.

Purpose: To demonstrate how different types respond to stressful situations and an opportunity to glimpse the inferior functions. The idea here is that under stress we show our true type.

Time: 30 minutes

Materials: Double row of chairs to represent a lifeboat.

Process: (1) Get eight volunteers of different types. Try to get people with clear preferences. Have them sit in the chairs backwards (if possible) so that a sense of uneasiness is created.

(2) Give the following instructions. "You are in a small lifeboat, and the boat is about to sink because there are too many people in it. Two have to go overboard. Those 2 have no chance of survival because of cold water and sharks. The group must work out who goes overboard."

Give a time limit. (Ten minutes till boat sinks.)

Hints about how the types may respond

ESFJs may ask if any have families; NTs may look at options, think they should draw straws; INFPs, ENFPs may offer to jump (gives life meaning and significance); and ESTPs may start scheming to get others to jump (female: I'm pregnant!). NFs almost always choose to jump (give life meaning, know that this isn't it, I'm just going on to other options, something better).

---

(3) Have the 2 jumpers leave the boat. Ask those who stay in the lifeboat to make a speech, then make a final comment to the group and to the jumpers. Then have the jumpers do the same.

(4) Debrief with the group, discussing the decision-making process and noting similarities and differences between people. Discuss which of these are related to type and which are not.

Developed by Eve Delunas.

Murder Mystery

This exercise was originally designed to show how information is communicated in problem-solving groups. However, when some of the necessary information was accidentally omitted, its use as an exercise to demonstrate type differences became apparent.

Purpose: To demonstrate how the four dominant functions work in problem solving, and the special role of the dominant Intuitive.

Time: 30 to 40 minutes

Materials: Clues (listed on page 88) on separate pieces of paper, enough for each group to get one copy of each clue.

Process: (1) Break participants into small groups; ideally each group has 9 participants, two of each dominant and one observer.

(2) Give each team a complete set of clues except for the two motive clues, which are NOT given. Each clue is on a separate piece of paper and is passed out randomly to group members. Each participant receives several clues.

(3) Instruct the participants to use the clues to identify the murderer, weapon, and place of the murder, and the murderer's motive. Participants may share their clues verbally, but may not show them to each other.

(4) Each group should have at least one observer. The observers are given the solution and told what to observe as evidence of the different functions at work. They may look for different possibilities, logic of approach, or specific facts noted. They also note any complaints about the exercise and who does or doesn't participate.

(5) When the separate groups have solved the murder, assemble the whole group and ask for observers' comments. Then give participants the opportunity to discuss how they felt during the process and why they pursued certain lines of inquiry.

The instructor may contribute to observations made during the exercise.

Developed by Kaaren Jacobson. (Reprinted with permission from *TypeWorkS*.)

Published by the Center for Applications of Psychological Type

Clues for Murder Mystery Exercise

- When he was discovered dead, Mr. Thompson had a bullet wound in his calf and a knife wound in his back.

- Mr. Barton shot an intruder in his apartment building at midnight.

- Mr. Thompson had virtually wiped out Mr. Barton's business by stealing his customers.

- The elevator operator reported to police that he saw Mr. Thompson at 12:15 a.m.

- The bullet taken from Mr. Thompson's calf matched the gun owned by Mr. Barton.

- Only one bullet had been fired from Mr. Barton's gun.

- The elevator man said Mr. Thompson did not seem too badly hurt.

- A knife found in the parking garage had been wiped clean of fingerprints.

- Mrs. Scott had been waiting in the lobby for her husband to get off work.

- The elevator man went off duty at 12:30 a.m.

- Mr. Thompson's body was found in the park.

- Mr. Thompson's body was found at 1:20 a.m.

- Mr. Thompson had been dead for about an hour when his body was found, according to the medical examiner.

- Mrs. Scott did not see Mr. Thompson leave through the lobby while she was waiting.

- Bloodstains corresponding to Mr. Thompson's blood type were found in the basement parking garage.

- Police were unable to locate Mr. Barton after the murder.

- Mr. Thompson's blood type was found on the carpet outside Mr. Barton's apartment.

- There were bloodstains on the elevator.

- Mrs. Scott's husband did not appear in the lobby at 12:30 a.m., the end of his normal working hours. She had to return home alone and he arrived later.

Hints about how the types may respond

Usually dominant Intuitive will guess the motive almost immediately, but the Intuitive's observation is dismissed without serious consideration by the group. Then one of two things happens: the group fails to come to a consensus about the motive or finally gives in to the Intuitive just to end the exercise. But the other dominants are usually not convinced of the motive.

The dominant Sensing type's typical complaint is that there isn't enough information to decide a motive, and they may even want to stop the exercise because of lack of information.

The dominant Thinking types attempt to draw conclusions about the motive based on logic. Since no logic can explain the motive suggested by the Intuitives, it is dismissed out of hand.

The dominant Feeling types often do not engage themselves much in the exercise, perhaps because the exercise does not call for any assessment of values. When Feeling types do attempt to determine motive, they usually involve their feelings about the characters in their judgments.

Clues left out:
- Mrs. Scott had been a good friend of Mr. Thompson and had often visited his apartment.
- Mrs. Scott's husband had been jealous of the friendship.

Murder Mystery Solution:
After receiving a superficial gunshot wound from Mr. Barton, Mr. Thompson stepped on the elevator and was killed by Mr. Scott (the elevator man) with a knife at 12:30 a.m. because Mr. Scott was jealous.

Magic Shop Fantasy Trip

Purpose: To demonstrate how and why different types make value judgments.

Time: 30 minutes

Materials: None.

Process: (1) Tell participants to do the following:

> I would like you to imagine you are in a forest, a lovely forest. Close your eyes and imagine it. I'd like you to imagine that in this forest you are very surprised to discover a building, a lovely little building, very unique looking, with your name over the door and the words "Magic Shop." Upon investigating, I'd like you to imagine that you find a dwarf who lives there. He introduces himself, welcomes you, and tells you that, "Yes, indeed, this is your Magic Shop."
>
> "What makes it magic," he says "is that these are all intangibles on the shelves of the shop; intangibles are things you can't touch, such as peace, love, intelligence, honesty, and success." He gives you the opportunity to choose one thing from the shelves of your magic shop and to take as much as you desire.
>
> The dwarf will want something back for what you are taking away— something desirable, not something bad. Take only one thing, in any amount you wish. But give back as much as you took.

Decide what you want to take from the shop and what you will give back. You must give back something you value, though not as much as the thing you take. You must give up as much of that item as you take of the other item.

Note: If there are a lot of Sensing types, you may need to give a much longer list of intangibles since they don't think about intangibles as naturally.

(2) After giving the participants time to think this over, have them discuss it in unlike or type-alike dyads or groups.

Hints about how the type may respond

Feeling types may choose love or harmony. Thinking types may give love for knowledge.

Variation: This exercise may be done in a fishbowl or it may be done as a fishbowl *first*, and then as a small group exercise.

Developed by Eve Delunas.

Personality Clash on a Management Team

Purpose: To learn how type might be related to personality conflicts.

Time: 20 to 30 minutes

Materials: Flip-chart paper and markers.

Process: Read or paraphrase the following scenario to participants:

> *Two members of a management team frequently seem to have misunderstandings. Mr. Green is often the idea man of the team, suggesting with enthusiasm that the team try this or that. Generally his ideas seem sound to the team, but are in need of refinement and attention to practical details. White, another team member, is usually the first one to question Mr. Green's ideas, on grounds of practicality, and she states her position in such a blunt way that she sometimes causes hard feelings. At that point, Mr. Green clams up and his idea fades away without the team dealing further with it. Outside of team planning meetings, Green and White seem to get along quite well.*

Analyze the Green-White relationship by answering these questions:

(1) What types are Green and White (make a guess)?

(2) How can you explain the conflict in terms of type theory?

(3) Assuming you are a member of their team and felt a need to help them, what would you say? Write your remarks just as you would say them, using quotation marks.

(4) Do you identify with either Green or White more than with the other? Would you be comfortable in the role of peacemaker between these two? Do your responses to these questions relate to your own type?

Adapted from *People Types and Tiger Stripes*, copyright 1996 by Gordon Lawrence. Used with permission.

Published by the Center for Applications of Psychological Type

A Play History

Purpose: To become aware of the leisure/play patterns within an individual's life and relate those to type; to question and evaluate desired future play behaviors.

Time: 30 to 45 minutes

Materials: Handout of the "Favorite Activities List" or a posting of this list on a chalkboard, flip-chart paper, or overhead.

Process: (1) Ask each participant to write a play history and then process the activity with the entire group.

(2) Ask participants to examine their lists and answer the following questions:.
- HOW have your activities CHANGED?
- WHAT patterns can you see?
- DO these PATTERNS relate to TYPE?
- What FUNCTIONS are expressed in your most recent activities?
- Are your current activities SPILLOVER or COMPENSATORY?

(3) Ask them to note play activities they would like to include in the future.

Developed by Judith Provost.

Favorite Activities List

List your favorite activities/pastimes for the following ages:

Childhood

1) _____

2) _____

3) _____

High School

1) _____

2) _____

3) _____

College

1) _____

2) _____

3) _____

Age 20–30

1) _____

2) _____

3) _____

Age 30–40

1) _____

2) _____

3) _____

Age 40–50

1) _____

2) _____

3) _____

Age 50–60

1) _____

2) _____

3) _____

Age 60–70

1) _____

2) _____

3) _____

Age 70–80

1) _____

2) _____

3) _____

Published by the Center for Applications of Psychological Type

Be an Object

Purpose: To demonstrate type differences.

Time: Depends on number of participants.

Materials: None.

Process: (1) Tell each participant to choose an object in the room and be that object. Give them five minutes to think about or experience being the object. Then have them each speak about why they chose that object, and what it means to be that object. In other words, to talk about themselves as that object.

(2) Have the other people listen for type descriptions in the explanation of the object.

> ### Hints about how the types may respond
>
> **INFP** – (as a purse) private, no one gets to see inside me; I have secret pockets, valuable treasures inside.
>
> **ENFP** – (as a sprinkler system) so sensitive to heat and cold; help protect others.
>
> **ENTJ** – (as a sprinkler system) hard, strong; reminder that I can protect under all circumstances.
>
> **ENTJ** – (as a desk) big, strong, with lots of file drawers.

Developed by Eve Delunas.

Be Your Mate (Boss, Parent, or Sibling)

Purpose: To hear the other person's frame of reference; to see type combinations at work; to hear pluses and minuses of types.

Time: 15 to 20 minutes

Materials: Need to know the other person's type in advance.

Process: (1) Ask everyone to stand up. Tell them they are transformed into someone they know very well: a spouse, ex-spouse, sibling, parent, boss, best friend (e.g., Mary becomes her spouse, Jim).

(2) Ask participants to randomly choose someone in the workshop and to introduce themselves as this other person and tell the assumed person's type. (Mary introduces herself as Jim to someone else and tells his type.) The other person in the pair will do the same. They should each then tell two things they like about their spouse and two things they don't like. (Mary, as Jim, tells two things that Jim likes about Mary and two things Jim doesn't like.)

(3) Then the participants should find *another* person to introduce themselves to and repeat the whole process. For the next 5 to 10 minutes, people should mingle and introduce themselves to as many people as possible.

Developed by Eve Delunas.

Published by the Center for Applications of Psychological Type

Mystery Guest

Purpose: To practice observing type characteristics.

Time: 20 to 30 minutes

Materials: A person who knows his or her type, but whose type is not known to the others in the group.

Process: (1) Introduce the mystery guest by name. The guest should sit in a position where everyone can observe him or her.

(2) Tell the group that they are going to try and discover the person's type by asking questions. They may ask any questions except those on the MBTI instrument (or "What type are you?"), and the guest must answer them honestly.

(3) After 10 minutes, stop the questioning and ask how many people think they have identified the guest's type. Have them tell what type they believe the guest to be and why. Then discuss why the guesses are right and/or why they are wrong.

(4) Remember to explain that while guessing is fun and often useful for good communication, people should never stereotype or pigeonhole another's type.

Developed by Eve Delunas.

Parenting the Difficult Child

Purpose: To understand different parenting styles as related to type.

Time: 20 to 30 minutes

Materials: None.

Process: **(1)** Have 2 people of different types come up to the front of the room. Tell them that they are to play themselves, but to pretend they are married and have an ESFP child.

(2) Ask an ESFP to volunteer to play the ESFP child, or ask someone to pretend that he or she is an ESFP if there isn't one in the group. Tell the group that the ESFP child comes home having just gotten in trouble with the law. Tell the parents to deal with the child. Type differences will usually emerge even though the people are aware that others are watching.

Hints about how the types may respond

INTs say, "Lets wait until we are all calm. We can discuss it logically in the morning."

ENFPs may be the rescuer: "You must feel bad that this happened"; or they may be off-the-wall hysterical.

ESTJ may say "How could my child do this to me? I must have failed as a parent! I feel terribly irresponsible; you must feel irresponsible." They may begin lecturing.

---

(3) You may want to do this exercise with several different triads and then discuss differences and similarities as a large group.

Developed by Eve Delunas.

Published by the Center for Applications of Psychological Type

Relationships

Purpose: To show how type works in interactions with others; to help participants think about how to use type to get along with others.

Time: 30 minutes

Materials: None.

Process: (1) Divide participants into male-female pairs. Some of the pairs should be type-alike, some should be type different.

(2) Have the dyads discuss what it would be like for the two of them to be married. Ask them to consider which positive things associated with this type combination would be satisfying and pleasing to each. Also, address what the weaknesses of this combination would be and which aspects would likely cause friction.

(3) Ask each dyad to report its findings to the whole group.

Variation: This exercise can also be cast as pairs that work together.

Developed by Eve Delunas.

What's in a Letter? The Mnemonics Exercise

To those quite familiar with type, a set of four letters, such as ENFP, conveys a quick picture of not just those four preferences but also of the type that emerges when they interact. The characteristics of these combined preferences can be hard to remember for people new to type. This exercise offers participants a chance to compose meaningful descriptions of whole types. This method uses mnemonic devices, which are memory aids that assign meaningful words to difficult or seemingly meaningless combinations of letters.

Purpose: To deepen understanding of types through attaching meanings to the four letters as a whole.

Time: Approximately 15 minutes

Materials: Flip-chart paper and markers.

Process: This exercise can be done individually or in groups or pairs of the same types. If you do not have the right mix for same-type pairs or groups, one option is to mix different types and have the group work in turn on each member's type.

(1) Explain what mnemonics are and show some examples.

Examples of type mnemonics:

Inside **N**eed **F**or **P**eace

I Serve **F**amily **J**oyfully *

Everyone **S**eems **T**oo **P**roper *

I'm **N**ot **F**ully **P**resent

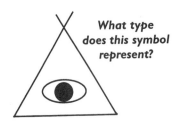

What type does this symbol represent?

(2) Ask each individual or group to assign words to the four letters of its type so that the totality of the words describes that personality type. Then each person or group should record its mnemonics on the flip-chart paper.

(3) Have each individual or group present its mnemonics. Post the mnemonics for reinforcement or reference. Encourage participants to share additional mnemonics if they can.

Answer: INTP (eye in a tee pee)

*Reprinted with permission from Hirsh, S. K., & Kummerow, J. M. (1989). *LIFEtypes*. NY: Warner Books.
Reprinted with permission from *TypeWorkS*.

Published by the Center for Applications of Psychological Type

Parenting

Purpose: To demonstrate differences between type preferences, especially those related to values.

Time: 20 to 30 minutes

Materials: Flip-chart paper and markers.

Process: (1) Divide participants into groups. Depending on the number of participants, divide participants into type-alike, cousin type, or function groups.

(2) Ask them to answer the question, "How would you know if you've been successful as a parent?" Have each group come up with its answer in only one sentence. Have each group write its sentence on the flip-chart paper. (Note that for some types a single sentence is impossible!)

(3) Have each group report back to the whole group. As each group reports, point out similarities and differences in what was discussed and recorded. Look for value differences.

Developed by Eve Delunas.

Type Verification Dialogue

Purpose: To help clarify differences between preferences; to help individuals verify their types.

Time: 30 to 60 minutes

Materials: *Dialogue Worksheets* handout (*Let's Talk and Waves of Discovery*)(available from CAPT).

Process: (1) After initial discussion about a preference pair, ask for 2 volunteers to read the *Let's Talk* dialogue aloud.

(2) Following the dialogue, ask participants to place a mark on the side of the waves that seems to fit them best at this point.

(3) Repeat for each preference pair.

(4) Ask participants to compare the guesses on the *Dialogue Worksheets* with their MBTI results.

Developed by Candice Johnson.

Published by the Center for Applications of Psychological Type

Resources

Reading List

TypeWorkS. A bimonthly newsletter for people who use type in organizations, published by Kay Abella from 1994 to 2001. Although the newsletter is no longer in publication, copies of articles and issues are available through the Isabel Briggs Myers Memorial Library at the Center for Applications of Psychological Type in Gainesville, Florida. Contact library@capt.org.

Delunas, E. E. (1981). *A potpourri of group exercises for teaching about type.* Presented at MBTI-IV, the Fourth Biennial National Conference on the Use of the Myers-Briggs Type Indicator, Palo Alto, CA.

TYPEtype. The official newsletter of the New Zealand Association for Psychological Type

Type Description Resources

The following publications, available from CAPT, include full descriptions of the sixteen types and can be very useful when explaining type:

Demarest, L. (1997) *Looking at type in the workplace.* Gainesville, FL: Center for Applications of Psychological Type.

Hirsh, S. K., & Kise, J. A. G. (1997). *Looking at type and spirituality.* Gainesville, FL: Center for Applications of Psychological Type.

Lawrence, G. D. (1995). *Descriptions of the sixteen types.* Gainesville, FL: Center for Applications of Psychological Type.

Lawrence, G. D. (1997). *Looking at type and learning styles.* Gainesville, FL: Center for Applications of Psychological Type.

Martin, C. R. (1995). *Looking at type and careers.* Gainesville, FL: Center for Applications of Psychological Type.

Martin, C. R. (1997). *Looking at type: The fundamentals.* Gainesville, FL: Center for Applications of Psychological Type.

Myers, I. B. (with Myers, P. B.). (1995). *Gifts differing: Understanding personality type.* Palo Alto, CA: Davies-Black. (Original work published 1980)

Page, E. C. (2005). *Looking at type* (5th ed.). Gainesville, FL: Center for Applications of Psychological Type.

Page, E. C. (1993). *Una mirada a los tipos psicológicos [Looking at type].* (R. Moody, trans.). Gainesville, FL: Center for Applications of Psychological Type. (Original work published 1987, 1992)

Organizations

American Association for Higher Education (AAHE)

One Dupont Circle, Suite 360
Washington, DC 20036-1110
(202) 293-6440
FAX (202) 293-0073
E-Mail: info@aahe.org
Website: www.aahe.org

American Counseling Association (ACA)

5999 Stevenson Avenue
Alexandria, VA 22304-3300
(800) 347-6647
(703) 823-9800
FAX (800) 473-2329
Website: www.counseling.org

American Psychological Association (APA)

750 First Street, NE
Washington, DC 20002-4242
(800) 374-2721
(202) 336-5500
Website: www.apa.org

American School Counselor Association (ASCA)

1101 King Street, Suite 625
Alexandria, VA 22314
(703) 683-2722
FAX (703) 683-1619
E-Mail: asca@erols.com
Website: www.schoolcounselor.org

American Society for Training & Development (ASTD)

1640 King Street, Box 1443
Alexandria, VA 22313-2043
(800) 628-2783
(703) 683-8100
FAX (703) 683-1523
Website: www.astd.org

Association of Psychological Type (APT)

9650 Rockville Pike
Bethesda, MD 20814
(800) 847-9943
Website: www.aptinternational.org

Center for Applications of Psychological Type (CAPT)

2815 NW 13th Street, Suite 401
Gainesville, FL 32609
(800) 777-2278
(352) 375-0160
Website: www.capt.org

Published by the Center for Applications of Psychological Type

National Board for Certified Counselors, Inc. (NBCC)
3 Terrace Way, Suite D
Greensboro, NC 27403-3660
(336) 547-0607
FAX (336) 547-0017
E-mail: nbcc@nbcc.org
Website: www.nbcc.org

National Education Association (NEA)
1201 16th Street, NW
Washington, DC 20036-3290
(202) 833-4000
Website: www.nea.org

National Association for the Education of Young Children (NAEYC)
1313 L Street, Suite 500
Washington, DC 20005
(202) 232-8777
FAX (202) 328-1846
E-Mail: naeyc@naeyc.org
Website: www.naeyc.org

Society for Human Resource Management (SHRM)
1800 Duke Street
Alexandria, VA 22314
(800) 283-SHRM
(703) 548-3440
FAX (703) 535-6490
E-mail: shrm@shrm.org
Website: www.shrm.org

Klein Group Instrument™
For Effective Leadership and Participation in Teams

CAPT is pleased to announce the soon-to-be-released **Klein Group Instrument,** an outstanding tool to assess the ways in which an individual successfully contributes to the efforts of a team.

Research has shown that teams function at their best when four key areas are addressed by the group as a whole. The **Klein Group Instrument** reflects this research and is constructed around the scales of

- leadership,
- negotiation orientation,
- task focus, and
- interpersonal focus.

The author and creator of the KGI™, Robert R. Klein, received his doctorate from Harvard University in the study of group behavior, and he has spent more than 12 years developing, researching, and testing this dynamic new instrument.

Once the KGI is released, you and your clients will be able to take the instrument online.

KLEIN

Out of the Box
Exercises for Mastering the Power of Type to Build Effective Teams

How often have you wished for the perfect set of exercises complete with ready-to-go handouts for a class or seminar?

Out of the Box by Charles R. Martin and Thomas J. Golatz provides just such materials for working with teams and small groups in refreshing and unique ways.

Combine your expertise and teaching skills with the resourceful and professionally crafted exercises in this book and you will have a formula for success!

Charles R. Martin and Thomas J. Golatz
2003. CAPT. 165 pages.
Workbook Binder with CD-ROM
Product No. 50304

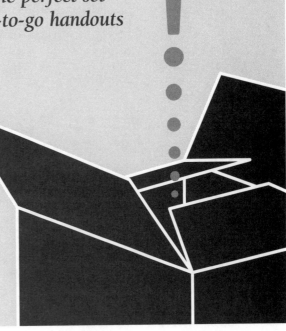

Published by the Center for Applications of Psychological Type

TRAINER'S TOOL BOX

1. A *Looking at Type® PowerPoint® CD-ROM*, describing type through easy to understand language and newly designed situational graphics. Each adds a fresh and fun approach to any introductory MBTI® presentation.

2. The *Looking at Type® Talking Points* script, designed as a companion piece for the CD-ROM, is easily customized with the addition of personal examples.

3. The *Looking at Type®* introductory booklet reflects the content of the CD-ROM and is included as a sample handout for future program participants.

4. *Looking at Type®: The Fundamentals*— a 60-page book written for the person new to psychological type, including basic information on type theory, extensive descriptions of the 16 types, and information on how type can be applied in everyday life.

5. *Sample MBTI® Training Handouts* —a preview binder that includes samples of more than 40 handouts to support trainers and consultants in a variety of workshop settings.

6. *Shape Up Your Program*—a book of more than 60 tried-and-true exercises developed by well-known and experienced MBTI professionals.